Supporting Numeracy

Supporting Numeracy

A Guide for School Support Staff

Ashley Compton, Helen Fielding
and Mike Scott

Paul Chapman Publishing

© Ashley Compton, Helen Fielding and Mike Scott, 2007

First published 2007

Apart from any fair dealing for the purposes of research or private study, or criticism or review, as permitted under the Copyright, Designs and Patents Act, 1988, this publication may be reproduced, stored or transmitted in any form, or by any means, only with the prior permission in writing of the publishers, or in the case of reprographic reproduction, in accordance with the terms of licences issued by the Copyright Licensing Agency. Enquiries concerning reproduction outside those terms should be sent to the publishers.

Paul Chapman Publishing
A SAGE Publications Company
1 Oliver's Yard
55 City Road
London EC1Y 1SP

SAGE Publications Inc
2455 Teller Road
Thousand Oaks
California 91320

SAGE Publications India Pvt Ltd
B-42 Panchsheel Enclave
PO Box 4109
New Delhi 110 017

Library of Congress Control Number: **2006932893**

A catalogue record for this book is available from the British Library

ISBN 13 978-1-4129-2890-8
ISBN 13 978-1-4129-2891-5 (pbk)

Typeset by Pantek Arts Ltd, Maidstone, Kent
Printed in Great Britain by Athenaeum Press, Gateshead, Tyne & Wear
Printed on paper from sustainable resources

Contents

Preface	vii
1 Mathematics or numeracy?	1
2 Language and mathematics	12
3 Mental methods	24
4 Number	36
5 Shape, space and measures	50
6 Data handling	65
7 Problem-solving	79
Appendices	93
References	107
Further reading	111
Index	113

Preface

This book has been written for people supporting mathematics in primary schools. It is of particular interest to those undertaking a Foundation Degree or pursuing Higher Level Teaching Assistant (HLTA) qualification. The role of the teaching assistant (TA) has grown considerably in recent years and, as a result, much higher levels of skills and knowledge are required to fulfil this role effectively. This book will help to raise your skills and knowledge about supporting mathematics by explaining the underlying concepts and the underpinning research. Common misconceptions are considered, alongside suggestions about how to support children of all abilities. Case studies from practising teaching assistants are used to put this all in context. As well as addressing the primary mathematics curriculum, some wider issues are explored.

A key feature of this book is the inclusion of research summaries. These should help you to understand the reasoning behind the teaching strategies and help you consider how children learn. However, research articles are often written in very technical language. The summaries are designed to make these more accessible but they are also intended to encourage you to read further about the topic. The references and further reading sections provide suggested texts to deepen your understanding. To use this book effectively it is important to undertake the tasks and reflect on your own experience in the light of what you have read.

Opportunities for teaching assistants to attain recognition as professionals are increasing as their profile is raised. Part of this process for some is gaining recognition as a Higher Level Teaching Assistant. To do this TAs must meet published standards. This book includes activities for reflection and discussion which are related to these standards. The intention is to provide a framework within which TAs can explore ideas related to these competencies. It should be made clear that fulfilling the activities will hopefully be good preparation for TAs intending to follow the HLTA route, but will not provide a comprehensive route to meeting the standards without other input.

The authors have all taught mathematics across the primary age range and currently are senior lecturers in higher education. They teach primary mathematics across a wide range of programmes including undergraduate and postgraduate teaching qualifications, and the Foundation Degree in Educational Studies for Teaching Assistants.

Exercises, extensions to tasks and other useful information can be found in the appendix section at the back of the book.

The authors would like to thank the following teaching assistants who so kindly allowed us to include case studies taken from their Foundation Degree assignments:

Emma-Jane Bowden
Lorna Garfoot
Anne-Marie Goode
Kerry Hugill
Tracy Mountford
Lynn Pope
Donna Young

Patricia Fox
Katy Green
Samantha Heeley
Jacqueline Johnson
Tamsin Nash
Amanda Wright

1

Mathematics or numeracy?

> This chapter will help you to:
>
> - improve your understanding of the mathematics involved in real-life situations
> - appreciate the value of putting mathematics in context
> - understand the structure and principles of the numeracy strategy

What is mathematics?

As adults when we reflect on our experience of learning mathematics through primary and secondary school, we tend to think of it in compartments in terms of the lessons and topics we encountered. If asked to list them, many adults would suggest that mathematics is arithmetic, geometry and algebra, maybe statistics or calculus. We might consider mathematics as being divided into pure or applied mathematics. However, mathematics can also be considered in a broader sense, involving problem solving, searching for patterns and communicating ideas.

Mathematics is one of the core subjects in the primary school curriculum, along with English and science. It is a government recommendation that it is taught every day and it is viewed as an essential life skill.

What is numeracy?

The term numeracy has been widely adopted in primary schools recently, rather than mathematics. Numeracy is a recently coined term, being a contraction of 'numerical literacy'. It has been defined in a variety of ways such as the ability to use mathematics or the application of mathematics in other areas of the curriculum.

In the National Numeracy Strategy it was defined as:

> ... a proficiency which involves confidence and competence with numbers and measures. It requires an understanding of the number system, a repertoire of computational skills and an inclination and ability to solve number problems in a variety of contexts. Numeracy also demands practical understanding of the ways in which information is gathered by counting and measuring, and is presented in graphs, diagrams, charts and tables. (DfEE, 1999: 4)

This definition focuses on the content of what is being learnt and taught in the different areas of mathematics. Numeracy, as a term, seems to reflect the way in which children approach their mathematics, valuing the confidence in and understanding of mathematics. The National Numeracy Strategy suggests that 'the outcome should be numerate pupils who are confident enough to tackle mathematical problems without going immediately to teachers or friends for help' (DfEE, 1999: 4). The term numeracy seems to reflect the competence level of the mathematics to be learnt with more of a focus on the skills to be achieved.

Mathematics in everyday life

Consider the complexities of selecting a suitable mortgage from the baffling selection available, probably one of the biggest financial decisions most of us ever need to make. We need to be certain of the options on offer so we can select the one which will be beneficial and affordable, taking into account all the possibilities available. Having a clear understanding of mathematics is socially empowering so we are not at the mercy of those who are more mathematically astute.

> **TASK 1.1**
>
> *HLTA 1.6 Be able to improve your own practice through observation, evaluation and discussion with colleagues.*
>
> Take a few moments to note down where you have used or encountered mathematics over the last 24 hours. This could involve calculations, making estimations, using measurements including time, handling data or working with shapes. Discuss how you have used maths knowledge most with a colleague. See Appendix 1 for some ideas.

Simply arriving on time for work or school involves many mathematical skills, for instance the ability to tell the time, read a timetable, calculate the time needed to walk a certain distance or, in the process of driving, estimate the speed of the oncoming traffic and use your spatial awareness to reverse into a parking space. Every shopping transaction involves a mathematical decision, even if it is just, 'Can I afford this?' This is known as *functional numeracy*, having sufficient mathematical knowledge to cope effectively on a day-to-day level (De Villiers, in Goulding, 2000: 140). We also need a *practical* understanding of mathematics; this comes into play when we are trying to redecorate a room or plan a new kitchen. This includes the ability to measure accurately and to calculate the area of floors or walls for buying carpets or tins of paint.

Ways of learning mathematics

If you think about how you undertake the everyday mathematics discussed above, it probably involves informal methods and estimation rather than the formal methods you were taught at school. These will be discussed further in Chapters 3 and 4. Working as a Teaching Assistant, you may have found that mathematics teaching today is very different from when you were at school. Some of this is due to research demonstrating that there are different ways of learning mathematics and different types of learner.

Research summary – Mathematical understanding

Skemp (1989) considers mathematical understanding to be of two forms: relational and instrumental. Relational understanding is having the ability to see the connections and relationships between numbers and areas of mathematics and to be able to apply them to new situations, 'knowing what to do and why' (Skemp, 1989: 2). Instrumental understanding involves the learning of mathematical rules and being able to carry them out effectively. Most mathematical learning is a mixture of these two ways of understanding and there are times in the learning of mathematics when both are appropriate and useful. Each has its value but having a relational understanding gives a depth of understanding and the opportunity to apply it. Most teachers seek to develop this understanding in their pupils and it is certainly encouraged in the National Numeracy Strategy framework. The ability to make connections is vital in learning in all subjects, especially the link to prior understanding, which helps to put new learning in context. Throughout this book the connections between the different aspects of mathematics will become more apparent.

Further work on different types of mathematical understanding has been undertaken. Two types of cognitive styles were identified by Bath and Knox (1984) and developed further by Chinn (1997) (both cited in Henderson et al., 2003: 25). These are identified as grasshoppers and inchworms; their characteristics are described in Table 1.1.

Table 1.1 Learning style characteristics

Inchworm learners	Grasshopper learners
Are prescriptive	Are intuitive thinkers
Like facts	Like 'the big picture'
Write information down	Make estimates
Look for formulae	Look for patterns
Avoid verifying	Like to verify information
Follow procedures	Solve problems mentally
Use a single method	Make flexible use of methods which change
Use numbers exactly as given	Adjust numbers for ease of calculation
Enjoy analysis	Enjoy investigations

Much of Chinn's work considers children with dyslexia and looks at ways to support different types of learners. However, these cognitive styles are appropriate for all learners of mathematics, whether children or adults. As with relational and instrumental understanding, we all use a combination of both styles, often depending on the situation.

> **TASK 1.2**
>
> *HLTA 2.5 Know the key factors that can affect the way pupils learn.*
>
> Try the following question noting the method you use:
>
> $2 \times 3 \times 4 \times 5 =$
>
> Now consider the characteristics listed above and try to identify aspects of a particular style which you employed. In very general terms those who favour an inchworm style undertake the question beginning at the start and perform each step in order so as to be certain of completing the question. Grasshoppers tend to select numbers which are initially easier to multiply, often finding pairs of numbers and then finally multiplying them together. For example, 2×5 and then 3×4, followed by 10×12.

Chinn (1997) has found that most people use a combination of both styles and it may depend on the question asked, though some questions favour a particular learning style. There can be difficulties with both ways; for instance, those who favour an inchworm approach may struggle if they are unable to remember a method or strategy upon which they rely, whereas grasshoppers need to learn to document their work so they can keep track of their thinking and their work can be understood and any errors identified.

Having a connected understanding of mathematics aids the understanding of new concepts and reinforces those already established. It helps us to begin to think mathematically. 'Thinking mathematically is not an end in itself; rather a process through which we make sense of the world around us' (Mason et al., 1982, in Tanner and Jones, 2000: 104). It is important to consider the value of the mathematics being taught and learnt and to put this into a context which will be meaningful to the learner.

When revisiting negative numbers with adult students, an abstract question such as 'minus fifteen subtract five' can cause confusion when reflecting on half remembered rules. However, when the question is rephrased in terms of an increasing debt, for example 'You are already £15 in the red and you spend £5', the question becomes more accessible and therefore solvable. In order to be effective, a real-life example needs to connect to children's actual experience and be as close as possible to their real world. Many suggested examples in published schemes tend to be unrealistic, sometimes just using words from everyday life in a word problem. This will be discussed further in Chapter 7.

Research summary – Street mathematics and school mathematics

An interesting example of the learning of mathematics in a real-life context was a study undertaken by Carraher et al. (1993) in Brazil. Their intention was to determine the effectiveness of traditional mathematics instruction in the elementary school versus mathematics learned informally through working. Their focus was children working as market traders in Recife, Brazil.

Much of the researcher's time was spent shopping in the street markets undertaking the same transactions at each stall; this was designed to measure particular arithmetical skills which were being taught in school. These same questions became part of a paper and pencil exercise undertaken with the same children in school. One of the examples included in the study is the purchase of four coconuts which cost 35 *cruzeiros* (Cr$) each. The twelve-year-old boy replied: 'There will be one hundred five, plus thirty, that's one thirty-five . . . one coconut is thirty-five . . . that is . . . one forty' (Carraher et al., 1993: 24).

When facing the question in the market setting, the boy began by breaking the problem up into simpler ones based on his prior knowledge which was that three coconuts cost Cr$105. Then, to add on the cost of the fourth coconut, he first rounded the cost of a coconut to Cr$30 and added that amount to give Cr$135 and added in the correction factor to give the answer Cr$140. However, when facing the same question in the school situation his response was 'Four times five is twenty, carry the two; two plus three is five, times four is twenty.' He then wrote down '200' as his answer. Here he has applied a formal algorithm for column multiplication, although as he was able to maintain the positions of the places the respective numbers would occupy, he was unable to apply the necessary carrying rule resulting in a much larger price. While he was able to answer this question in the real setting, he did not apply this knowledge or an appreciation of the magnitude of the anticipated answer in the school setting.

The study gives many similar examples from other children who worked as market traders showing the interesting situation where children could calculate when the mathematics was presented in a real-life situation which they could relate to (street mathematics) but not when presented in a standard arithmetic form. There was a purpose to the street mathematics, where the question makes sense and has meaning, in direct contrast to the standard symbolic approach taken in the elementary school. The findings from this study make very interesting reading and reinforce important issues for mathematics teaching in all countries. One of the most important is the value of putting mathematics in an appropriate and realistic context for children (and adults) to make sense of, so they can apply their understanding more effectively by being able to construct appropriate meanings to all the abstract concepts and methods they will encounter in school.

TASK 1.3

HLTA 3.1.3 Contribute effectively to the selection and preparation of teaching resources that meet the diversity of pupils' needs and interests.

Consider the areas of mathematics which you have encountered most recently. Were there examples of real-life situations linked to the mathematics undertaken? For example, the children were learning about addition. Were all the questions just straight calculations or were they set in the context of real-life problems? Can you think of ways to develop, extend or include real-life opportunities into these sessions?

Public perceptions of mathematicians

There is growing concern over the diminishing numbers of children choosing to study mathematics at a higher level. Fewer pupils select to take their A levels in mathematics leading to a lower take-up for degrees in mathematics. Secondary schools are finding that there are fewer qualified teachers of mathematics. There are a great many reasons for this, one of which being the wide range of subjects offered in universities which are attracting larger numbers of students. Another is the way that mathematics and mathematicians are perceived by society.

Research summary – Children's perceptions of mathematicians

In the 1950s a pilot study was undertaken by Mead and Metraux (cited in Chambers, 1983) to discover the attitudes young people held towards science and scientists in order to ascertain why they were not following previously popular careers in science, especially engineering. This was the Draw A Scientist Test (DAST) later developed by Chambers (1983). Through this they could discover the views and images held by pupils. It was found that very stereotypical views were held of bespectacled men in lab coats.

A similar range of studies has been undertaken examining views of mathematicians, usually focusing on children of 12 and 13 years of age. Berry and Picker (2000) conducted a study comparing children's drawings of mathematics in the UK and the USA. In more than 300 responses from both countries, the majority of drawings showed white males, similar in nature. A range of themes emerges from the drawings, generally strongly negative stereotypes. The following is just a selection of comments which annotate the drawings. 'Mathematicians have no friends, except other mathematicians. They are usually fat, unmarried, aren't seeing anyone, and have wrinkles in their forehead from thinking so hard' (2000: 25). In the UK, Carol Vorderman from *Countdown* appeared occasionally as the sole representative of a female mathematician. The image portrayed, as with the scientists, is not a good one and inevitably reflects society's view. When asked about the employment of mathematicians, calculating taxes or working in a bank were suggested. Some suggested that teachers may be mathematicians and the drawings reflect this, but they did not generally consider their own teacher as such. It would seem from the study that many young people hold a negative view of mathematicians and feel far removed from those people they perceive as mathematical. Other studies have been undertaken in Finland, Germany and Romania which have generated very similar findings.

In recent years mathematicians have featured in major films: *A Beautiful Mind*, *Good Will Hunting* and *Pi* present three distinct images of mathematicians. Even so, these figures are all men and each suffers from one form of instability or another. These too are hardly strengthening the mathematical image.

As teachers of mathematics we need to avoid perpetuating a negative image of mathematics and mathematicians. Despite any earlier experiences we may have had in our own school careers which discouraged us or made us doubt our own abilities, it is important we do not demonstrate these feeling to the children we are working with. Society often reflects these negative feelings towards mathematics; it is socially acceptable, even funny, to acknowledge that you are not good at maths in a way that you would not dream of saying about other subjects. Our attitudes to different subjects are strongly influenced by our parents and our teachers. We can all remember enjoying a particular subject because we could relate to the teacher or because they made their subject interesting through their own enthusiasm for it. It is important then to portray a positive approach to mathematics which will be infectious to the children you are working with.

The following case study shows the value of putting mathematics in an exciting context and making the objectives accessible to the children.

Case study 1.1 Anne Marie Goode: Choosing a suitable context for mathematics

In groups of three, the children were asked, firstly, how many skittles there were (ten), secondly, to tell me what number was printed on each skittle (randomly), and then to set the skittles up in the way they thought would allow them to knock over the most skittles at one time. They then took turns to roll the ball and knock some of the skittles over, which brought us to the main aim of the activity. The children would count how many skittles they had knocked down and then how many were left standing, thus leading them to the conclusion that, for example, 'ten take away four leaves six'.

With closed questions, such as, 'How many are knocked over/left standing?' some of the children needed to count the skittles individually each time to give me an answer, while others remembered the calculation from a previous turn. A few of the children could sometimes tell me the calculation without counting the skittles from previously learned facts. For example, J told me that $10 - 5 = 5$ without even looking at the skittles. When I asked him how he knew that, he answered, matter of factly, 'because $5 + 5 = 10$'. He already was inverting addition and subtraction. R told me she had nine left standing when she knocked one down, 'because 9 is one less than 10'. Nevertheless, the closed questions did seem to convey a somewhat limited response.

The open-ended questions on the other hand led to some very interesting discussions. Although a few of the children were quite vague with their answers – for example, when one child was asked how she knew a particular answer, her reply was 'I just know' – the majority of them were happy to elaborate and get involved in a discussion. The open-ended questions allowed the children to hear other points of view and explanations and ultimately learn from each other's responses and strategies.

With a different group of children I used an activity from the National Numeracy Strategy's Springboard 3 programme. This game appeared to have a very positive impact on the children's comprehension of the place value concept. Throughout the activity the children and I maintained a constant conversation pertaining to the task and the methods used to complete it. I also asked a range of open-ended questions which were recommended in the programme, for example 'How do you know which is the largest and which is the smallest number?' or 'How do you know that the numbers are in the correct order?' The children took great delight in answering the questions correctly and, depending on how the questions were delivered, it appeared at times as though they were actually telling or teaching me something. I feel that this strategy works wonders for raising the self-esteem of these children, who in a whole-class session will not answer for fear of being wrong and therefore humiliated in front of their peers.

> **TASK 1.4**
>
> *HLTA 3.2.2 Monitor pupils' responses to learning tasks and modify approach accordingly.*
>
> Reflect on the strategies employed in this activity. Identify those which helped to make this a positive and accessible experience for the children. See Appendix 1 for further comments.

The National Numeracy Strategy

The National Numeracy Strategy (NNS) was introduced into English primary schools in September 1999, following a period of individualised learning in the 1970s and 1980s, when many resources were published that were aimed at children working at their own rate. The view was generally held that children would benefit from an almost individual programme and that this approach offered differentiation. While children were working on these schemes, there was little direct teaching and many children were not able to progress as the materials were not at a suitable level. Although there were guidelines already in place in the form of the National Curriculum (DFE, 1995), there was seen to be a need to give schools more specific guidance. The 'Three Wise Men' report (Alexander et al., 1992) proposed that more whole-class teaching would be effective, rather than individual teaching and the use of published mathematics schemes which were favoured by many schools. In the Trends in International Mathematics and Science Study (TIMSS) for 1995, ten-year-old children in England were found to be performing at a lower level than those in many other countries, especially those in the Pacific Rim. This difference was particularly apparent in areas of mathematics such as mental arithmetic and basic number skills (Mullis et al., 1998). These all contributed to the formation of the National Numeracy Project which evolved into the National Numeracy Strategy.

While the framework of the NNS was not statutory, there was strong pressure for schools to adopt the guidelines as this would be a focus of OfSTED inspections. The NNS framework made specific recommendations to schools. The opening paragraph of the section titled *'Teaching Mathematics'* gives a broad overview. The approach to teaching recommended by the NNS is based on four key principles:

- dedicated mathematics lessons every day;
- direct teaching and interactive oral work with the whole class and groups;
- an emphasis on mental calculation;
- controlled differentiation, with all pupils engaged in mathematics related to a common theme.

(DfEE, 1999: 11)

These principles can be seen to be a direct result of the reports mentioned above and the findings of the first series of OfSTED reports, where elements of good practice in primary schools were identified and incorporated into the guidelines.

The introduction of the National Numeracy Strategy has raised the profile of mathematics in the primary school and has raised the standards in most aspects of mathematics. In the TIMSS report for 2004, England was acknowledged as one of six countries which have made a significant improvement since 1995; the report considers the progress of English ten-year-olds who now appear 36 points above the international average (Mullis et al., 2004: 212) compared to 16 points below in 1995. However, the strategy was reviewed in 2006 in order to continue to raise standards. Methods and resources for teaching and learning mathematics continue to develop and it is important for those who are working with children to keep abreast of developments in mathematics, such as the use of ICT.

Mathematics in the age of technology

It is tempting to think that it is no longer necessary to teach mathematics to the same degree in the present technological age, where calculators and computers can calculate so quickly and accurately. However, it is probably more important to have a confident level of understanding in mathematics in order to function successfully in today's society. The place of calculators will be discussed in Chapter 3.

Computers have been used in British primary schools for approximately 30 years. Changes in equipment and programmes available are rapid and many children are already familiar with the use of PCs, as a high proportion of families have a computer at home. In recent years the use of interactive whiteboards, laptops and stand-alone PCs, as well as digital photography and many other resources, has increased in the primary school.

There is a huge range of resources available commercially. As with all resources these need to be selected with care to ensure they are of an appropriate level, are suitably engaging and are value for money. They are rather variable in quality. There are many excellent web-based materials which can be used effectively with an interactive whiteboard. The Interactive Teaching Programs (ITPs), available on the Primary National Strategy website, are particularly effective and are linked to specific learning objectives. They are designed to support the daily mathematics lesson, enabling the teacher or teaching assistant to give a focused input. The use of the interactive whiteboard means that all children can be involved and individuals can interact directly with the program, providing a teaching and learning opportunity. Many of these are very adaptable and can be used in an open-ended way.

Effective use of ICT in the teaching of mathematics has been reported by OfSTED and HMI (cited in Moseley et al., 1999). They suggest that using ICT as a demonstration and as a modelling tool with the whole class is particularly effective. A variety of working methods are also appropriate: focused small-group work perhaps with a teaching assistant; work with the whole class working in pairs in computer suites in order to practise skills modelled by the teacher. ICT is already used widely across the curriculum and its use is likely to increase. However, it is important to remember that ICT should be used to support the teaching and learning of a specific learning objective and should not be used for the sake of it.

> **TASK 1.5**
>
> *HLTA 2.4 Know how to use ICT to advance pupils' learning, and use common ICT tools for your own and pupils' benefit.*
>
> Make a list of the ICT resources (equipment and programs) that your school uses to support mathematics. What mathematical concepts are addressed? What are the advantages of using ICT instead of another method?

> **Key Points**
>
> - Mathematics is an essential life skill.
> - Presenting a positive attitude towards mathematics promotes more effective learning.
> - The use of appropriate ICT resources can be a powerful tool for enhancing learning.

> **Reflections**
>
> What are your experiences of mathematics?
>
> How will you portray a positive image of mathematics to the children?
>
> Do you need to develop your confidence in using ICT to support mathematics?

2

Language and mathematics

> This chapter will help you to:
>
> - recognise the role of language in mathematics
> - identify difficulties that children have with mathematical language
> - appreciate the importance of spoken, as well as written, language in mathematics

For many adults the idea that language has a large role in mathematics may seem quite odd. They may have memories of sitting silently in rows while completing pages of 'sums' neatly lined up in columns. However, this is not the case today. The National Numeracy Strategy (DfEE, 1999) promotes the use of language in the different parts of the daily mathematics lesson. From the inception of the NNS there was a mathematical vocabulary book to accompany the framework which suggested how language, and especially questioning, could be used. Since then, the Primary National Strategy has produced materials on speaking and listening (DfES, 2003a) emphasising their importance across the curriculum, including in mathematics.

This chapter will consider how language contributes to understanding mathematics, especially in the form of discussion. Some of the problems presented by mathematical language will be demonstrated and the importance of planning for the use and understanding of language in all parts of the lesson will be emphasised.

Research summary – The Cockcroft Report

The Cockcroft Report (Cockcroft, 1982) was the result of a major investigation into the teaching and learning of mathematics in Britain. It used statistical analysis, international comparisons, observations and anecdotal evidence to arrive at a range of recommendations about teaching mathematics at the primary and secondary levels. One issue that was highlighted by the report was the role of language in mathematics. Near the beginning of the report the committee stated, 'We believe that all these perceptions of the usefulness of mathematics arise from the fact that mathematics provides a means of communication which is powerful, concise and unambiguous' (Cockcroft, 1982: para. 3). Like many government reports, paragraphs or sections are used rather than page numbers in references. The other paragraphs related to language (paras 11, 246, 306–10) are summarised below.

Cockcroft recommended that there should be many opportunities for discussion in mathematics lessons, not just question and answer sessions, from the earliest days in school. However, children start school with different levels of mathematical language and understanding and this must be taken into account. Although children usually learn to speak their native language easily, learning to communicate using mathematical language is harder. One difficulty is that some words, when used in mathematics, have different meanings in everyday language. For example, the word 'difference' to indicate subtraction is one that often causes problems (see Chapter 4). 'Take away' can also be used to indicate subtraction but may make the children think of Chinese or Indian food.

Precision is important in mathematical communications and so correct vocabulary must be both learned and practised. Children need to become familiar with the variety of expressions that can be used to indicate different operations. However, you need to be careful with this since sometimes these expressions can be misleading. For example, the word 'more' can indicate an addition or a subtraction question depending on how it is used.

The report also advised that mathematics lessons should include practical activities and discussion. Explicit links should be made between related areas of mathematics through discussion since even able students do not notice these easily. Another important suggestion was that those people who find mathematics easy should recognise that other people find it very difficult and may need much help in learning it.

Although the Cockcroft Report was published in 1982, many of the issues are still current and will be discussed in this chapter and other parts of the book.

> **TASK 2.1**
>
> *HLTA 2.2 Be familiar with the school curriculum.*
>
> Consider the issues summarised above. Which of these do you recognise as being issues in your school today?

Can there be learning without language?

Before they can speak babies start to explore the world around them with their senses. If you study a young child exploring shapes with a posting ball you can witness the learning even though no language is involved. The child looks at the shape, feels the shape and often even tastes the shape before trying to post it through the holes. The first attempts are very hit and miss but gradually, with repeated exposure, the child learns which shapes will fit into which holes and that some can be posted in a range of orientations. It is important to remember this example when you encounter children who are struggling with mathematics due to the language involved. They may need to be supported with opportunities to explore the concept physically before they can understand the more abstract concepts through language.

Research summary – Language and number

Gelman is a major researcher in the development of mathematical understanding and is well known for developing the counting principles for young children (see Chapter 4). The two papers (Gelman and Butterworth, 2005; Gelman and Gallistel, 2004) summarised below looked at adults and children and how the presence or absence of mathematical language affected number concepts.

Some people believe that learning requires language, a theory known as 'linguistic determinism'. Research with animals, very young babies and people with language difficulties has challenged this theory because the research has shown that mathematical ideas exist and, in some cases, can be developed despite a lack of language. The alternative theory promoted by Gelman and her colleagues is that language allows us to express concepts we already have but may also influence our developing understanding of those concepts.

Studies were undertaken with Pirahã and Mundurukú Indians from Brazil because the languages spoken by these cultures had either no number words or only number words for 1 and 2. The tasks, which were non-verbal, included simple addition, subtraction and ordering with numbers up to 80 and relied more on estimation than precise counting. The results showed that the Brazilians tested had a similar understanding of estimation to European adults.

There are two effects which have an impact on how people interpret number when estimating rather than counting. The size or magnitude effect means that it is easier to compare two numbers if they are both small. For example, it is easier to compare two objects to three objects and say which has more than to compare 29 objects to 30 objects. The distance effect means that it is easier to compare numbers if the numbers are far apart rather than close together. For example, it is easier to compare two objects to six objects and say which has more than to compare two objects to three objects.

The fact that the magnitude and distance effects were present in both the Brazilians and Europeans tested indicates that the lack of number language did not have an effect on the estimation process. However, the results did show that those people without number language did not have the same sense of the exact quantity of numbers that is demonstrated through counting.

The conclusion is that some mathematics can exist without language but that number words and/or notation may help develop an understanding of the exact property of numbers.

Mathematical language

Language is very important in helping us to categorise concepts and make connections. The study of the Brazilian Indians demonstrated that a lack of mathematical language resulted in an imprecise sense of number. When trying to categorise and make connections precise use of language is vital. In Chapter 5 the importance of using language precisely to name and describe shapes will be demonstrated.

Often there is a conflict between mathematical use of language and everyday use. For example, you will hear some people describe a shape as being a diamond (see Figure 2.1). The word 'diamond' is not a mathematically defined shape so what do they mean? Generally they mean a square that is poised on a corner with a diagonal parallel to the page edge. Sometimes they mean a different form of rhombus. Occasionally they are referring to a kite. They could even be referring to the shape of a multi-faceted cut diamond that is used in rings and on quality marks.

Figure 2.1 Which is the diamond?

Imagine that the person using the word diamond is talking on the telephone so the person on the other end cannot see the shape being described. The use of the word diamond has not helped the other person understand what the shape looks like. Using the word diamond to describe a square that is placed on its corner also leads children to believe that part of the definition of a square is that the base must be parallel with the page.

> **TASK 2.2**
>
> *HLTA 3.3.2 Communicate effectively and sensitively with pupils to support their learning.*
>
> You need a partner for this task. Draw an arrangement of three or four shapes but don't let your partner see it. Describe your arrangement as precisely as possible so your partner can draw it. When done compare the drawings. Keep taking turns drawing and describing different arrangements until they are reasonably accurate. See Appendix 2 for some common responses.

One way of developing mathematical language is through Logo, a computer programming language that requires very precise use of mathematical language or it will not work. It is often used in a basic form with floor turtles such as Roamer, Pixie and Bee-Bot that can be used by young children. The instructions must be given in the correct order to make the robot move to the desired location. Initially this is done in 'direct drive' with children inputting an instruction and then seeing where the robot goes. However, this can be developed into sequences of instructions, including repeats. More complex versions of Logo are available on computer with a screen turtle. They are excellent for developing children's understanding of shape and space but can also be used for introducing algebra. High-attaining children can be challenged to use variables and more advanced algebra in an interesting context with Logo programs.

> **Case study 2.1 Amanda Wright: Imprecise use of mathematical language**
>
> Another problem is adults as well as children use mathematical words imprecisely. One of my own children has used the phrase, 'I'll have the bigger half.' This is mathematically impossible. I have used the term, 'wait a minute' when I really mean five minutes and so confuse the child about lengths of time. The word 'nothing' to express a zero is a particular problem when teaching place value.

The diamond example shows the difficulties that can occur because of conflicts between mathematical language and everyday language. There are many words used in mathematics that have subtly different or completely different meanings in everyday language. Shuard and Rothery (1984) devised three categories: technical words (only have meaning in mathematics, e.g. circumference); lexical words (have similar meaning in everyday English, e.g. remainder) and everyday words (have similar and different meanings in everyday English, e.g. difference, volume).

> **Case study 2.2 Pat Fox: Everyday words**
>
> *There are 14 socks on the washing line. How many pairs of socks?*
>
> One child asked what a 'pear' had got to do with socks. I asked him to try and explain. He said, 'What's fruit got to do with socks?' I asked the rest of the group if they could explain what a pair meant in the question. They were able to say that we have pairs of socks and shoes. I then had to ask how many was in a pair; only one child put his hand up. I asked them to think about where shoes were worn and asked them to guess. Another child put her hand up and gave me the correct answer, saying we have two feet, so it must mean two.

As noted in the Cockcroft report (Cockcroft, 1983: para. 308), there are other problems posed by mathematical vocabulary. The four main operations in mathematics (addition, subtraction, multiplication and division) can all be described by many different words. Think about addition: how much, how many, total, sum, altogether, add, plus. Can you think of any more words? The *Mathematical Vocabulary* book (DfEE, 2000) is useful for exploring the range of words used for different operations. It is important to note that the word 'sum' is defined mathematically as the answer to an addition question, although it is used much more widely by most people to mean any sort of mathematical question.

Pronunciation can also cause difficulties in mathematics. This is particularly a problem in the early years when many children's speech is still developing. It is also a problem for children with hearing difficulties and ear infections. A common mistake is confusing or mishearing 'teen' and 'ty'.

> **Case study 2.3 Samantha Heeley: Pronunciation of numbers**
>
> One pupil answered a question with 19 when the answer was in fact 90. The pupil was asked to explain how he came to this conclusion. He explained his strategy and the answer but again stated 19 as opposed to 90. Once this misconception was highlighted he was given extra support on the basic pronunciation of numbers.

Research summary – Spoken language and mathematics

Language is used throughout mathematics lessons in many ways. As well as specific mathematical vocabulary, it is used for instruction, explanation, demonstration, questions, discussion, social interaction. This means that difficulties with language can impede mathematical understanding in various ways.

The fact that mathematical vocabulary often has a different or more precise meaning than everyday language causes problems for teachers as well as children. Studies have shown that many teachers are uncertain of the correct mathematical vocabulary and their underlying concepts – possibly because it was taught badly to them.

Raiker (2002) found that the teachers used more mathematical words than the children in nearly all cases. Children used more mathematical words when participating in whole-class discussions with the teacher than when working in small groups just with other pupils. However, all three groups (teacher, pupils in whole-class situations, pupils in small groups) used lexical words most and technical words least.

Although the teachers stated in the interviews that teaching key vocabulary was important, none of the lesson plans showed how the key vocabulary would be taught. In the lessons observed there was no systematic teaching of key vocabulary, there was little repetition of the key vocabulary by the teacher and the terms were often used in an imprecise and confusing manner. Raiker recommends that lesson plans should highlight key vocabulary and explicitly state how it will be taught to the pupils so that its meaning is clear.

The children did use some of the key vocabulary during whole-class discussions with the teacher but rarely when working in small groups with their peers. However, Raiker noted that the children in small groups used language to explore the mathematical concepts and develop their own and their peers' understanding. The language used by the children in these small group situations helped to demonstrate their thought processes, misconceptions and perceptions of their own level of understanding. She noted that these conversations, and the assessment opportunities they presented, were often missed by the teacher.

One of the advantages of being a teaching assistant is that you have more opportunities to work with small groups and individuals and witness the sort of conversations described above. It is important that you take note of these conversations to help you assess the children's understanding.

> **TASK 2.3**
>
> *HLTA 3.1.1 Contribute effectively to teachers' planning and preparation of lessons.*
>
> Can you think of any mathematical terms you have used imprecisely? What impact does this have on the children's understanding?
>
> Make a list of all the mathematical words you can think of that could be confused with everyday words. You might want to include words that sound the same even though they are spelt differently, e.g. sum and some. See Appendix 2 for some 'problem' words.
>
> For the next mathematics lesson that you are involved in make a list of the relevant mathematical vocabulary. Check that you understand the mathematical meaning of each word. Plan how you could explain them to children.

Language in the daily mathematics lesson

There are many opportunities to use spoken language in the daily mathematics lesson. The oral and mental starter is an obvious example, given the name. However, it is important to monitor if the pupils are speaking or if it is just the teacher talking. Some schools use talking partners. The talking partners can be used to discuss ideas about the problem or just the final solutions. Sometimes the talking partners are used to offer the other person's answer to the class. This can be helpful with pupils who are reluctant to offer their own answers due to shyness or fear of being wrong.

There are many strategies for encouraging children to answer without having to say it aloud. Many schools use number fans or place value cards for children to show their answers. Many use an updated version of the Roman wax tablet or the Victorian slate – the individual whiteboard. These strategies allow the teacher to see quickly if everyone has been able to answer the question but reduce the amount of speaking time for the children. They also prevent the more able or vocal children dominating the session without discouraging them from answering.

As well as just giving their answers, children are encouraged to explain their methods. This is true in all sections of the daily mathematics lesson and is an issue that will be discussed in more depth in the next chapter. The act of explaining to someone else often helps us to clarify the idea in our own heads and reinforces the learning. However, many children find it difficult to explain their methods and it is important that explaining methods is modelled for them by adults and other children.

Listening to their explanations can give the adult useful assessment information about their understanding of mathematics. Do not be surprised if you find it difficult to understand a child's method. When explaining children often leave out important steps that make the explanation difficult to follow. It can help if the child demonstrates the method in writing or images as well as orally. Gifted and able children sometimes choose particularly convoluted methods to challenge themselves.

As well as modelling how to explain methods, adults need to explain mathematical concepts and problems. Frequently these explanations need to be reworded in several ways before all of the children can understand the concept. Applying the concept to a real-life situation is helpful.

> **Case study 2.4 Tracy Mountford: Rephrasing**
>
> Children with Special Educational Needs (SEN) may often rely heavily on language to help them. A case study of a nine-year-old girl who has SEN shows this. Sarah has a particular problem with numeracy and often has to have things explained to her over and over again. Many of the people who work with her often try rephrasing explanations until she is happy with one she understands. One particular lesson Sarah was shown this problem:
>
> $6 \times 12 =$
>
> She pondered over this for some time before saying she was unable to answer. Then it was explained to her like this:
>
> A lady went to a supermarket to buy some beans to feed her family. She bought six trays of beans and each tray contained twelve tins. How many tins of beans did she have altogether?
>
> Sarah began to draw six trays with twelve tins. Once she had done this she then counted all the tins individually and eventually came up with the answer. Although this was a long way to answer this question she was able to attempt to answer it confidently whereas before she didn't know where to begin.
>
> Teachers or teaching assistants often have to put mathematical questions into real-life situations. As with most subject areas children are confident in what they know. This is why giving problems real meaning helps children answer; this is especially the case in numeracy.

As well as rephrasing and setting into a context, visual images can be useful in developing children's understanding.

Research summary – Mental images and language

Bills (1999) was interested in studying the mental representations that the pupils had in their heads when they were calculating. Bills observed one lesson per week, with a focus on the representations the teacher used to develop understanding of place value, and interviewed students in March and July. The interviews demonstrated that the children's explanations of how they answered questions gave clues about the mental images they were using. In seven of the nine cases interviewed both times the mental images the children used were the same in both interviews. This implies that these images became stable. There was also evidence that the mental images in children's heads were heavily influenced by the models and language the teacher used in the classroom.

The main part of the mathematics lesson often starts with a whole-class introduction. The NNS has produced some Interactive Teaching Programs (ITPs) that are available from their website (www.standards.dfes.gov.uk). Many of these are best used with a projector and interactive whiteboard to promote discussion during whole-class introductions. Key vocabulary can be emphasised and questions raised. One ITP about capacity shows a graduated cylinder that can have virtual liquid added to it or removed from it. The large projected image of the graduated cylinder allows the class to discuss how to read the scale, the size of step between each mark on the cylinder and what the different line lengths indicate. The large image ensures that the children can match the words related to the cylinder to the appropriate parts. The children can also make predictions and undertake calculations about adding and subtracting liquid from the cylinder, explaining their reasoning. One particular advantage of this ITP is that it allows you to change the scale, size of step, and start and end points easily. This lets you check if the children are able to apply what they learned from one graduated cylinder to another and helps to avoid unintended overgeneralisations (e.g. all cylinders go up in steps of 10 because this one does). While using the ITP the children could have their own cylinders and compare them to the one on the screen. Although the ITPs will never replace first-hand experience with the equipment, they augment it effectively and promote discussions.

The main activity part of the lesson may involve children working from textbooks or worksheets. Studies of mathematics textbooks in the past have found that there can be a mismatch between the reading level and the mathematics level. The repercussion of this is that many of the problems the children had were not about the mathematics but the result of not being able to read and understand the instructions. Even if the language level of the textbooks is at the same level as the mathematics, the same might not be true of your children. Children rarely develop evenly in all areas so it is not uncommon for a child to be better at mathematics than at reading and writing with the result that problems with reading and writing might be masking their true mathematical ability. This is particularly true of children with English as an additional language.

Language is not only spoken. Another important facet of children's mathematical communication is the written work they produce. This can mean the formal columns of calculations you may remember from your school days but it also includes more informal jottings and diagrams.

Research summary – Children's mathematical marks

Carruthers and Worthington (2003) are Early Years practitioners who studied children's mark making in mathematics both in the school and at home. They observed and recorded the children's mark making in everyday situations in the classroom, playgroup or at home, gathering over 700 samples from children aged three to eight years old.

They believe that it is important for early years practitioners to recognise children's informal mathematical marks so that these can be valued and developed as part of the transition to more formal mathematical marks and abstract work. When they interviewed Early Years teachers many of the informal mathematical marks were regarded as early writing rather than relating to mathematics.

From their research they determined that an important reason for encouraging children to make mathematical marks on paper is to aid the transition from the mathematics they have developed in their home life to the more abstract mathematics of school life. However, these mathematical marks need to be owned by the child rather than dictated by the adult. Extensive use of worksheets will work against this by forcing the child to record in a certain way. Some features that they found supported mathematical mark making were the use of open questions, providing blank paper and a variety of writing materials, and a range of models of mathematical marks from the adults and other children, including forms and graphs.

> **TASK 2.4**
>
> *HLTA 3.2.1 Be able to support teachers in evaluating pupils' progress through a range of assessment activities.*
>
> Collect a variety of examples of pupils' recording of maths. Do you feel comfortable with informal recording or does it feel that it is not 'real' mathematics? What do you think the purpose is for children recording mathematics?
>
> How were you required to record mathematics at school? Is this the method you use when doing mathematics for yourself?

There are many different reasons for recording in mathematics. It is important to think about who the recording actually benefits. Is it to help the child or just as evidence? In Chapter 3 the role of jottings to help children with mental calculations will be discussed. However, often recording in mathematics is done to provide evidence, for the school or the parents, that the child has completed the work. It can also provide an assessment opportunity if the child was working independently.

The last part of the daily mathematics lesson, the plenary, can involve children explaining their methods. An effective plenary activity is asking the children to explain which was the hardest question they did, which was the easiest and why. Children who find it difficult to express their thinking can be forewarned during the main activity that they will need to present their approaches in the plenary and then work with an adult on how to explain to others.

Language and making connections

Askew et al. (1997) found that the most effective teachers of mathematics were connectionists: those who made connections between different aspects of mathematics explicit. Making connections is an important part of teaching mathematics and requires that the adults involved know enough about mathematics to realise the connections between different areas. This is something that was not emphasised in the past so many adults are unaware of the connections themselves.

For example, many people do not recognise that fractions are just another way of expressing division and that the line in a fraction is another form of the division symbol. The denominator (bottom of the fraction) is the divisor and the numerator (top of the fraction) is the dividend. The quotient (result of the division) is the fraction expressed as a decimal number, for example $\frac{3}{4}$ is the same as $3 \div 4 = 0.75$. These concepts are also closely related to percentages, ratio and proportion.

From the above example you can see the importance of understanding mathematical concepts and mathematical vocabulary. The following chapters should help you develop both of these.

Key Points

- Discussion helps develop understanding of mathematics.
- Accurate use of language is important in mathematics.
- Lesson plans should specifically include relevant correct language and ways of teaching and reinforcing it.

Reflections

Are there some mathematical terms you need to look up to ensure you are using them accurately?

Do you plan for the introduction and reinforcement of mathematical vocabulary?

Do you encourage children to discuss their methods and record in their own manner?

Do you assess children's understanding from what they say as well as from what they produce?

Mental methods

> This chapter will help you to:
>
> - understand what is meant by mental methods and why mental strategies are important
> - develop your own confidence in using a range of mental calculation strategies
> - become familiar with some of the arguments about the use of calculators in schools

What are mental methods?

By mental methods we do not mean the quick recall of known facts. Instead we mean mental calculation strategies, ways of using known facts to solve problems 'in the head'. Some of these strategies involve making written notes ('jottings') at intermediate stages before arriving at the final answer, but mental strategies are not usually the same as formal written methods (the standard algorithms).

Older readers may remember when mathematics appeared to be separated into three distinct areas, 'mental', 'mechanical' and 'problems' (Thompson, 1999). Mental arithmetic involved weekly or even daily tests in which the teacher called out questions and children wrote down the answers as rapidly as possible. A quick response was a key feature of success.

In the 1960s and 1970s, teachers became increasingly aware of the range of ability in their classes and the effect of failure on the confidence of pupils. The difficulty in asking questions appropriate for all children, coupled with the increased availability and use of individualised workbooks, seems to have led to a decline in the use of mental work in the mathematics lesson. This was the situation described in *Mathematics Counts*, more commonly known as the Cockcroft Report (1982).

The report stated clearly the committee's belief that children should be able to calculate mentally (paras 254–6). It commented on the decline in the use of 'mental arithmetic' in schools and emphasised the importance of mental and oral work. The report also pointed out that the mental methods used by people in their daily lives were not straightforward versions of standard written methods, but were frequently adapted and individualised.

Cockcroft was very clear on the importance of not just mental calculation, but also the oral work or mathematical discussion which should accompany it (paras 315–20). This should include discussion between children as well as between teacher and pupil. In these paragraphs the report also states that young children should not start written work in mathematics too early; these ideas can clearly be seen now in the National Numeracy Strategy.

An emphasis on mental calculation is one of the four key principles of the National Numeracy Strategy (DfEE, 1999), and a range of strategies is suggested in the supplement of examples. These ideas are elaborated in *Teaching Mental Calculation Strategies* (QCA, 1999a), which provides very clear guidance for working with primary school children.

Thompson (1999) suggests that children need knowledge of number facts, an understanding of the number system, the skills to work with the numbers and a confident attitude which allows them to use what they know when faced with a problem.

The starter is a well known feature of the three-part lesson advocated by the National Numeracy Strategy. It usually takes five or ten minutes at the beginning of the lesson, and is intended to be a warm-up and to involve the whole class. It should get all the children alert and thinking mathematically, and while it must involve the whole class, questions need to be differentiated to target the different abilities of the children. Think of it in the same way as a PE warm-up; we would not take the class to the school hall then let two children run around while the rest watched. Every child should make some sort of response or contribution during the starter.

The starter is a time to practise previously taught skills, so the adult should not use it for teaching something new. However, it is not just a time for testing quick recall, but an opportunity to ask higher-order questions and use mental calculation strategies to solve problems. The known facts and skills that have been practised can then be used as stepping stones for calculation in the main teaching activity, where children use what they know and extend it.

Skilful questioning is an essential part of interactive mathematics sessions, and of developing children's mental calculation strategies. Questioning, including the hierarchy of questions, is discussed in Chapter 7, but of importance to this chapter is the idea of wait time, the time the adult waits for the child to give an answer. As adults we can find even the shortest pause between question and answer an uncomfortable silence which we feel must be filled. We are often too ready to intervene with prompts and rewording, when what the child needs is time not just to remember but to think. If we want to test a child's recall of a simple fact then expecting a prompt answer is appropriate; if we want the child to use known facts to work something out, then this requires a longer wait time. Not allowing wait time can increase stress and reduce a child's confidence and willingness to attempt answers.

Research summary – Wait time

There is some evidence from research observations that the wait time teachers leave is very short, perhaps as little as one second before the questioner intervenes (Cotton, 1988; Black and Harrison, 2001). According to Kyriacou (2005) the emphasis on rapid response, as seen in many lessons, hinders the development of 'strategic thinking' and a range of mental calculation strategies. Cotton (1988) found that for closed (lower cognitive) questions a wait time of three seconds was suitable but for higher cognitive questions children gave better answers the longer the teacher was prepared to wait. Reynolds and Muijs (1999) make clear that the appropriate wait time depends on the context of the questioning; higher cognitive questions need more wait time. Black and Harrison (2001) showed that teachers developing their use of wait time found it difficult at first not to intervene quickly, but got good responses from wait times as long as thirty seconds.

As pointed out in Chapter 2, children are encouraged to explain their methods. By putting their thinking into words and articulating their ideas, children become clearer in their own minds about the mathematics they are doing. Talking through the process and explaining to others is an excellent way to clarify thinking; you really have to understand a process to be able to explain it to someone else. There is a need therefore for discussion, between children as well as between teacher and pupil. The use of talk partners, encouraging children to discuss a question with their neighbour, is an effective strategy which allows less confident children to talk about mathematics without exposing themselves to the whole class straight away. Talk partners can be used in any part of the three-part lesson to allow both discussion and thinking time.

Children will develop mental calculation strategies best if they are not afraid to try ideas out in public. It is very important that the classroom or group ethos is one of trust, in which children know they can make suggestions without fear of embarrassment, knowing that ideas will be treated with respect. The supportive adult will help develop confidence by using positive comments, reminding children that they already possess useful knowledge and by ensuring that questions are pitched at a level that allows children to succeed while being appropriately challenged. Children's mathematical understanding will develop more strongly if they are willing to take risks.

Case study 3.1 Pat Fox: Using known facts

100 pencils are shared equally between 10 classes. How many pencils will each class get?

One child wanted to draw 100 pencils and I asked her if there might be another way of finding the answer. At first she was unable to answer. I then asked her to think about division and its relationship to multiplication. Still unsure I asked her, 'What calculation do you know with 10 and 100 in it?' She replied '10 × 10 = 100'. I then asked her to think back to what I had said earlier about multiplication and its relationship to division. She called out the answer 10. I asked her why, she replied, '10 × 10 = 100 so 100 ÷ 10 = 10. It's the opposite of multiplication.'

I asked the rest of the group how they had worked out the question. Apart from one, all had used their knowledge of the 10× table to find the answer. However, one boy had used a number line and jumped in steps of 10. When I asked why he said he was not sure of his times tables and had used this method. I praised him for his efforts and his clear description to the rest of the group. I asked the rest of the children if they thought this was a good method. They agreed that it was but if they knew the facts then it wasn't necessary but a good way to work it out.

The approach to mental methods needs to be flexible, as not everyone will use the same strategy for the same problem. Children need to be encouraged to use an individual approach which works; one of the skills of the teaching assistant is encouraging flexibility while engaging children in a discussion about which methods are most efficient.

Children should be encouraged to estimate when asked to solve a mathematical problem. It is important to have an approximate idea of what an answer should be, to give support to the calculated answer. This will be raised again in the section on calculators. An estimate is a 'thinking' guess, not a wild guess. Children should say, for example, that the answer to 97 × 5 will be 'a bit less than 500 because 97 is a bit less than 100'. Many children do not like to be wrong and find it hard to have an estimate that is different from the final answer. Some of you will have had children changing their estimate after completing the calculation. Again, a secure atmosphere, together with examples of how estimation helps, will develop children's confidence.

TASK 3.1

HLTA 3.2.3 Monitor pupils' participation and progress ... giving constructive support to pupils as they learn.

Observe some children solving a problem mentally. Discuss their strategies with them. Did they all use the same approach? Did any of them use estimation?

Mental methods

The National Numeracy Strategy *Framework* and the QCA book *Teaching Mental Calculation Strategies* provide a vast range of mental strategies that children should use at different ages. Only a few can be discussed here; some others are described in Chapter 4.

Number facts can be learned by exploration and explanation, then practised to make them secure. Complements of 10 are established using counters and partitioning them into two sets. When all the possibilities have been found (0 + 10, 1 + 9, 2 + 8, ... 9 + 1, 10 + 0) quick recall can be used to practise and internalise the facts. If these facts are combined with an understanding that addition can be done in any order (commutative and associative laws) then

7 + 5 + 3 can become 7 + 3 + 5
which becomes 10 + 5 = 15

This is explained further in Chapter 4.

Partitioning is the splitting of numbers into parts: 37 = 30 + 7, 146 = 100 + 40 + 6. It provides a useful strategy for addition or subtraction, for example 42 + 35 becomes 40 + 2 + 30 + 5. The tens and units can then be combined separately, 40 + 30 = 70, 2 + 5 = 7, then the tens and units recombined; 70 + 7 = 77, so 42 + 35 = 77.

Partitioning does not have to be into hundreds, tens and units; taking out fives can be a way of making a calculation easier. 7 + 5 becomes (5 + 2) + 5; then, because *addition can be done in any order*, (5 + 5) + 2 = 10 + 2; 10 + 2 = 12, so 7 + 5 = 12.

Both numbers do not have to be partitioned: 32 + 25 may be done as 30 + 25 + 2.

Knowledge of *complements of ten* allows the recognition of other partitioning: 6 + 7 = 6 + (4 + 3), which becomes (6 + 4) + 3; 10 + 3 = 13, so 6 + 7 = 13.

Some children would prefer to see 6 + 7 as a *near double*; double 6 is 12, 7 is 1 more than 6 so the answer is 13. It is equally valid to say double 7 is 14, 6 is one less than 7, so the answer is 13.

Bridging refers to counting on or back in two or more stages, using known fixed points as markers. Thus to calculate 47 + 25, the child might say 47 + 3 = 50, 50 + 10 = 60, 60 + 10 = 70, 70 + 2 = 72 (partitioning 25 into 3 + 10 + 10 + 2). This is called bridging through multiples of ten. A blank number line allows the start, intermediate and end points to be marked on as they are calculated. Bridging does not have to be through ten. To answer the question 'It is 08.40; how long is it to 09.15?' the child can bridge through 09.00; 20 minutes + 15 minutes = 35 minutes.

Some children may answer 47 + 25 by *compensating*; 50 + 25 = 75 (using known facts), but 50 is 3 more than 47, so 3 too many have been added on and 3 need taking off. 75 − 3 = 72. *Adding and subtracting 9 or 11* also involve compensating. Add or subtract 10, then add or subtract a further 1 to complete the calculation. To help understand this strategy, children benefit from plenty of experience with a number line or hundred square to see the relationships between the numbers.

In all these strategies the emphasis is on the calculations being done in the head, although notes may be made. This often involves working with the larger numbers, tens or hundreds, first, unlike the standard written methods which usually begin with the units.

> **Case study 3.2 Donna Young: Compensating**
>
> I decided to undertake an activity of using near numbers to complete an addition with a small group of Year 4 children. I wrote the calculation of 20 + 19 = on the board and asked 'What is the answer to this sum?' The response was quite delayed while some counted on their fingers and others just stared at the board working it out. This delay allowed me to suggest that there could have been an easier way. Asking 'How do you think we could make it easier?' did not prove successful so I changed this to 'Will it be under 50?' All of the children said yes simultaneously, yet they struggled to tell me why! I then had to do some prompting by asking them to look at the number 19 and asked them to consider what we could do with it to make it an easier number to add. One of the children said we could round it up to 20 to make it the same as the other number. When I asked him why he had said that, he said he just thought 19 was near 20. I then changed the number to 20. Doing this created a response of 'Now you've made it too big.' which I was pleased to hear because this was the stage I wanted to reach. I could now move my questioning to 'What is 20 + 20?' which they all knew. I then asked the children to look at what we had done and what we should do now. Another child said that we had added too much up because we were only supposed to add 19 so it was now wrong. I then asked how much bigger they thought it was. One of them said it was one too big. So I asked what we should do to make it smaller again. Most of them agreed that you would take one off.
>
> After practising a few more calculations using this method, I asked the children if they thought this method made it easier to do. Some felt it was easier. One child said she found it easier because when you add 20 + 19, you make it 40 in your mind because 20 + 20 was easier to do, then you take off 1 in your mind to get 39. Another said that her thumb was the 1 that she had added, then she added the new number and then her thumb told her to take the 1 off to make it right. This demonstrated that they had grasped the method and had devised their own strategy for this.
>
> Using open questions gave me more of an insight into what the children were thinking. The less able in the group were prepared to have a go at answering with the others because I was asking for what they thought they could do rather than a correct numerical answer. From my experience as a TA, lower ability children are often afraid to answer closed questions because of the fear of getting the wrong answer and subsequently feeling a failure.
>
> My role as a TA involved being flexible to the child's needs. From my experience, using open questions may take longer and can be frustrating but it gets children thinking rather than just guessing at answers to closed questions.

> **TASK 3.2**
>
> *HLTA 2.9 Know a range of strategies to establish a purposeful learning environment.*
>
> Look at the range of mental calculation strategies in the National Numeracy Strategy. Are there any which your children do not use which you think could be useful? How might you introduce them?

Mental calculation strategies cannot be developed without children having lots of practical experience and building up their own mental images. To assist in counting on and back, they need mental images of numbers and number lines; this can only be achieved if they have plenty of experience of using an actual number line. Children cannot be expected to visualise ten cubes, then take three away, if they have not actually handled and partitioned sets of cubes. DfES publications have made available a 'Models and Images' pack with a CD and a set of wallcharts which support the development of these mental images, and there are interactive teaching programs (ITPs) which can be used to demonstrate some useful calculation strategies.

During these mental calculations, some children will want to make notes or jottings to remember intermediate results; this is perfectly acceptable. The expectation of the National Numeracy Strategy is that children will move through jottings, to informal written methods, to standard written algorithms (the vertical written methods most adults were taught). However, standard algorithms should not be taught until children can confidently add and subtract pairs of two-digit numbers. Even when children are using formal written methods, mental calculation strategies should still be practised and used. Mental strategies should not be seen as a way of getting children on to standard written methods. Mental methods have their own validity and use, and must be taught, developed and refined throughout the primary school. Children need a very wide range of mental calculation strategies, as the appropriate strategy depends on the numbers involved in the calculation.

There can be a temptation when working with children with special educational needs to try and help them by teaching them the standard algorithms by rote, on the grounds that too many ideas will be confusing. In the mathematics classroom there is a tension between teaching conceptual understanding and teaching procedural fluency, the ability to 'do the method'. If we concentrate on procedure, then there may be short-term success but long-term understanding is likely to suffer. For children with SEN, if we teach them only the standard algorithms but even with lots of practice these are not retained, then the children will have no alternative method to use. Teaching a range of mental strategies gives children more choice.

Improving your own mental methods

In the past many schools put considerable emphasis on following a set procedure: the standard written algorithm. Following the steps and lining the numbers up neatly were viewed as far more important than understanding how to calculate. Some pupils even had their work marked wrong if they had the correct answer but did not use the approved method or did not show their working out. If this was your experience, you may lack confidence in your own mental methods. Some of the mental methods children are expected to use may be unfamiliar to you. The best way to become confident is to practise; as you use different strategies you will develop a wider understanding of the way numbers work and fit together. When attempting to solve a problem, think about what you know already, and how known facts can be used. Analyse your thinking and if possible compare your approach with that of a colleague.

Remember that maths does not have to be hard. If you are asked to give a pair of numbers that add up to 1000, there is no special virtue in saying 387 + 613; 999 + 1 is not cheating, it is just as valid and a lot easier. As your familiarity with numbers and the number system increases, so will your ability to find the most efficient strategies.

> **Case study 3.3 Donna Young: Analysing methods**
>
> *Answer the question 12.5 divided by 0.5.*
>
> When I looked at the question of 12.5 divided by 0.5 I immediately wanted to get rid of the decimal points so I had whole numbers to work with. I dislike decimals and making them whole allowed me to see more clearly and feel more confident with my working out. I visualised the decimal point moving one place to the right then I calculated 125 divided by 5, which was 25. I didn't say to myself 'multiply both sides by ten', yet that was the method I was undertaking.
>
> I asked several children from Year 6 how they would work the calculation out. I was surprised by how many different methods were used.
>
> Child 1 – I would count up in 0.5s until I got to 12.5
> Child 2 – I would count up in 5s up to 125 then put the decimal point back.
> Child 3 – It's like 50p so I would pretend it was £12.50 and then see how many 50p's there were in it.
> Child 4 – I would times it by 2 to make it 1, then it would be how many 1s in 25 which is 25.
>
> Child 2 had a similar method to me; child 4 had realised that multiplying both sides by the same number would make a whole number, which was also alike. All of the children did not hesitate in giving me their method; they were in no doubt about the way they would work the calculation out. Even if

it was not by my preferred method, I had to accept it was the one they were comfortable with. I asked the class teacher how she would teach this. She said that she would ask them to look at 0.5 as a half, then to calculate how many halves there were in 12.5. However, she was aware that children had different methods and would ask them for their own interpretations.

My findings made me more aware of my own practice as a TA. I realised that I probably didn't always ask children to tell me their methods. This was for reasons such as an eagerness to get on with the lesson because of time restraints, following teachers' instructions and believing that the method taught is the appropriate method for their ability.

TASK 3.3

HLTA 3.2.2 Monitor pupils' responses to learning tasks and modify approach accordingly.

Try these calculations mentally:

66 − 29, 66 + 8, 309 − 77, 309 + 95, 4.08 − 1.3, 4.08 + 3.1

180 ÷ 12, 25 × 7, 9.6 ÷ 0.4, 20 × 19

Analyse your own methods. What known facts did you use and what ideas did you apply? Would the children you work with do things the same way? See Appendix 3 for some methods.

The role of calculators

Since their introduction in the early 1970s, hand-held electronic calculators have steadily become cheaper, more available and more powerful. They have also provoked strong feelings. Cockcroft (1982) found widespread public concern about the use of calculators in school, though much less actual use than opponents feared. The report was very clear that calculators did not remove the need for mathematical understanding.

Research summary – Calculators

There was little overall impact on primary school mathematics until the 1980s when the Calculator-Aware Number (CAN) project was set up. This was a research project designed to investigate how children would respond to a number curriculum which actively exposed them to calculators. Specific classes within participating schools combined calculator use with mental strategies without teaching standard written methods.

Shuard et al. (1991) reviewed the progress of the CAN curriculum project. The authors were from the project team, so the report may be considered one-sided, but they did provide a lot of evidence for their findings. They also acknowledge the difficulties of comparing CAN and non-CAN pupils due to the level of support the project offered to schools and teachers involved.

Evaluators noted increased enthusiasm for mathematics from children and a greater confidence in solving problems by their own methods. Calculators were used for checking results and for doing calculations too difficult to be done mentally. Increased emphasis given to mental calculation meant that children were more confident to work things out in their head and knew when this was more appropriate than using a calculator. Discussion became an increasing feature of mathematics lessons, and children demonstrated a greater understanding of number patterns and relationships. When compared with other children, CAN children demonstrated equal or better performance in numeracy tests (Shuard et al., 1991).

However, in 1996 the Bierhoff Report (cited in Thompson, 1999) argued that calculator use was incompatible with mental calculation skills and that therefore calculators should not be used in primary schools. This was completely at variance with the findings of the CAN project, but was a popular view in some sections of the media and government.

The School Curriculum and Assessment Authority summarised a lot of available research and concluded that the use of calculators in most primary schools was 'modest' and their influence was 'relatively unimportant' (SCAA, 1997). The document drew attention to the range of other factors associated with curriculum initiatives involving calculators but said it was unlikely that calculators were responsible for poor mathematical performance in primary schools. The SCAA found that where schools had good policies on the use of calculators, pupils did not rely on calculators and had good attitudes to the use of mental calculation strategies.

Ruthven (1998) looked at the mathematical attitudes and the performance of Year 6 pupils in two groups of schools, one which had adopted a CAN type approach and one which had not. He gave children a series of mathematical problems to solve and analysed their responses. He found that children from the 'calculator aware' schools were more likely to use mental calculation strategies and had less recourse to calculators or written methods. Ruthven points out that a key factor in these schools had been the emphasis on, and direct teaching of, mental calculation strategies.

Calculators can be used for checking the answers to calculations, though we need to avoid any idea that the calculator is infallible. Children should, through prior estimation, be able to reject an impossible calculator answer brought about by incorrect key presses. Games in which mental skills are pitched against the calculator are a very good stimulus for developing mental strategies. A game in which children are only allowed to use, say, the 2, 3, 5, 7, +, −, = keys on their calculator to make all the numbers from 0 to 20 can develop addition and subtraction skills. Calculators can also be used for exploring number patterns, for working with large numbers and for complex calculations using real data.

> **TASK 3.4**
>
> *HLTA 3.1.3 Contribute effectively to the selection and preparation of teaching resources that meet the diversity of pupils' needs and interests.*
>
> Solve this calculation in your head: (19 + 18) × (72 − 67). Now solve it using a calculator. Analyse the difference. What knowledge, understanding and skills did you need in each case? Which method is more appropriate for you in this particular instance? See Appendix 3 for some ways of solving this.

It is a fact that calculators are widely available and in everyday use. Children need to be taught how to use them and to use them efficiently. This means they need to know not only how to press the right keys, but also to look at the display and know whether the answer is plausible. Mental calculation and estimation skills are essential, as already discussed, and the use of calculators does not make them redundant. One of the most important things to know about using a calculator is when it is more efficient not to.

> **TASK 3.5**
>
> *HLTA 3.2.1 Support teachers in evaluating pupils' progress through a range of assessment activities.*
>
> Ask some Key Stage 2 children to choose whether to do the following questions mentally or with a calculator:
>
> 350 + 150
> £12.95 + £17.95
> 100 − 36
> £5.00 − 95p
> £1.65 × 6
> 50p × 3
> £4.25 ÷ 8
> £5.00 ÷ 25p
>
> Look at the way the children use calculators. Do they try mental methods first? Are they always happy to accept the displayed answer? Do they estimate first to ensure the answer is sensible? Are they able to interpret the calculator display to give the answer? See Appendix 3 for some potential problems.

Mental calculation strategies are essential if children are to use mathematics confidently and efficiently. Some will be 'discovered' by children, and you need to be sufficiently informed and alert to pick them up. However, we cannot rely on chance discovery; strategies need to be taught. Not all will be appropriate for every child, but unless they have the opportunity to try a range of strategies they may not find the ones which are meaningful and easy for them. Without a good grasp of mental calculation strategies children will not have a sound understanding of number and the ability to develop and understand efficient written methods when necessary. The confident mathematician should be able to use a mental, written or calculator method as appropriate to the task.

> **Key Points**
> - Mental calculation strategies are essential if children are to use mathematics confidently and efficiently.
> - Mental calculation strategies need to be specifically taught and refined throughout the primary school.
> - A wide range of strategies allows children to choose the most appropriate method for them in any situation.

> **Reflections**
>
> Are you confident about using mental methods?
>
> How can you encourage children to use mental methods?
>
> How can we demonstrate to children that mental methods are at least as valuable as written methods?

Number

This chapter will help you to:

- consolidate your knowledge of place value and the four operations
- consolidate your knowledge of and the links between fractions, decimals, percentages, ratio and proportion
- recognise and address some of the common difficulties children encounter in the learning of these areas

This chapter will identify the key ideas and common misconceptions that children have in number, along with practical suggestions on how to address these. The main areas considered will be:

- place value and the number system;
- counting;
- four operations (+, −, ×, ÷)
  - standard algorithms
  - children's own methods;
- the relationship between fractions, decimals, percentages and ratio.

This chapter has a very wide brief and these areas of mathematics could easily constitute a whole book. Those who need more personal study to be confident using number should see the Further Reading section.

Before beginning to encounter numbers in school, children will have experienced numbers in a variety of different types of situations:

- cardinal numbers – used for a measure of size, quantity and for counting;
- ordinal numbers – used to show the order of a sequence, for example 1st, 2nd;
- nominal numbers – used as labels, for example house or bus numbers.

One of the earliest concepts in mathematics children encounter both at home and at school is counting. It is thought that children need a firm understanding of this before they can begin to add and subtract.

Counting

Knowing how many or how much is a vital aspect of our lives from an early age, so the *natural numbers* (1, 2, 3, . . . also called *counting numbers*) and zero are an important aspect of early mathematics. Counting, the ordering of whole numbers in a sequence, is a complex process and not as simple as it initially appears.

Research summary – Counting principles

Gelman and Gallistel (1978) identified the principles of counting, all of which are needed in order to count successfully. These principles may not all develop at the same rate.

- *Stable order principle*. The number names remain in a constant order. Many young children learn to count from a very early age as parents, siblings and teachers provide opportunities to learn the number order, particularly through songs and rhymes.
- *One-to-one correspondence*: Each item is to be counted only once. This is often done by touching, pointing, nodding towards or moving each object. This is an aspect which many young children find difficult, having learnt to count verbally almost as a list or a poem. Appreciating the correspondence between one number and one object may need reinforcing through structured and supported counting activities.
- *Cardinal principle*. The final number said indicates the number of items in the set. Children begin to realise that the last number name spoken is the answer to 'How many?' questions and tells you how many there are.
- *Abstraction principle*. Anything can be counted even if they are not exactly the same. This is the appreciation that counting the number of objects is not affected by their size or position or whether or not they are of the same type, for example counting dogs of different types and size or even a collection of dogs and cats.
- *Order – irrelevance principle*. Objects can be counted beginning with any item whatever its position within the set. Children begin to realise that no matter in which order a collection is counted the number remains the same.

There are two common ways in which children make errors when counting:

- The spoken or written sequence has errors in the order of the numbers being counted.
- One-to-one correspondence is not consistently applied so the cardinal number may be larger or smaller than the number in the set because occasional objects are double counted or missed out.

Children are less likely to make errors when counting actual objects rather than pictures that cannot be moved to indicate that they have already been counted.

Once children become secure in counting skills, the concept of more and less can be introduced, where the magnitude of numbers is directly compared. This usually begins with one more or one less, leading to the start of addition and subtraction. This is linked to the skill of comparing numbers without actually counting, called numerosity (referred to in Chapter 2), which is an innate skill found in very young children. Studies have shown that babies as young as a few days old can indicate the larger number when shown two and three objects or pictures (Antell and Keating, 1983).

Place value

Once the child is able to count to ten, an understanding of place value and the number system is needed in order to work with larger numbers in the context of primary school mathematics. The number system used in Europe is usually referred to as the 'Hindu-Arabic' system.

The early stages of place value involve the ability to order numbers and understanding that the position of a digit signifies its value. At a simple level it is the understanding that in the case of the number 957, the 7 is in the ones place and represents seven, the 5 is in the tens place and represents 50 and the 9 is in the hundreds place and represents 900. In all number operations the use of zero is vitally important as a place holder. This needs to be emphasised throughout all place value work and to be included as specific examples when practising the four operations.

There is a variety of useful resources to support the understanding of place value. Many schools use large hundred squares to demonstrate the relationship between the numbers. Overlapping arrow number cards (see Figure 4.1) and Dienes apparatus are also particularly helpful.

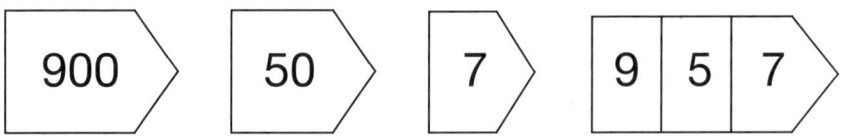

Figure 4.1 Place value arrow cards.

The four operations

As mentioned earlier, there is a great deal to understand about the four operations. In the following sections, the underlying structures of the four rules will be outlined. This helps develop an understanding of the connections between these operations and the different ways in which they may appear in the primary curriculum.

Each of the four operations is introduced following the same general pattern shown in the guidance to the National Numeracy Strategy. A suggested development is laid out in a very useful booklet, *Teaching Written Calculations* (QCA, 1999b).

Mental counting is introduced throughout the primary school from counting forwards and backwards in ones in the Foundation Stage and Year 1 to counting in decimals or negative numbers in Year 6. The early stages of mental calculation with written recording are introduced in Key Stage 1, through the learning of number bonds and developing strategies for working with smaller numbers, which usually involves horizontal recording. Towards the end of Key Stage 1 the use of informal jottings such as number lines will enable children to work with larger numbers. Number lines can be used for supporting learning in each of the four rules. For example, number lines are commonly used to represent multiplication, often in the form of number tracks or stepping stones. This provides a useful visual demonstration as equal jumps or arrows show the gradual build up of the product, as in Figure 4.2.

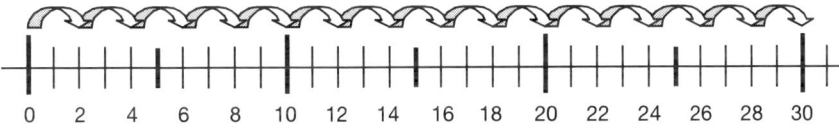

Figure 4.2 Multiplication with a number line.

Strategies such as adding or subtracting multiples of 10 or doubling and halving are introduced. During this development of methods, there will be the inclusion of a variety of informal methods. In teaching mathematics it is important to help children to begin to decide which methods are appropriate and efficient. For example, with 99 + 43 a useful method would be to consider the 99 as 100 then adjust the answer accordingly. However, a different two-digit number addition, 37 + 68, would lend itself more to other approaches such as a partitioning of tens and units: 30 + 60 = 90, 7 + 8 = 15, then 90 + 15 = 105; or partitioning and bridging through multiples of ten: 37 + 68 = 35 + 2 + 68 = 35 + 70 = 105. Although these methods look cumbersome on paper, they are easily done mentally and demonstrate a good understanding of place value and the number system, as discussed in Chapter 3.

These informal methods are followed by non-standard expanded written methods. These combine the strategies the child will already have developed and begin to lead into the standard algorithms which are more compact methods. Figure 4.3 shows examples of a non-standard expanded method for addition and a standard algorithm for multiplication.

```
        Addition              Mulitplication
         125                        37
        +467                        ×6
        ─────                      ────
          12                        42
          80                       180
         500                       222
        ─────                      ────
         592                         1
```

Figure 4.3 Examples of addition and multiplication.

This later introduction of the standard compact methods or algorithms is recommended until the children have a sound grasp of place value and have strong enough mental calculation skills to adopt these methods successfully. Without a good understanding of both place value and mental methods, children are unlikely to understand the standard algorithms and will probably struggle to apply them correctly. The standard written methods for the four operations which include addition with carrying and decomposition for subtraction, generally use a vertical column method which you probably learned at school yourself.

It is important that children appreciate the links between the four operations. The fact that addition and subtraction, and also multiplication and division, are inverse operations is an important aspect to promote understanding. For example, 3 + 4 = 7 so 7 − 4 = 3; 2 × 6 = 12 so 12 ÷ 6 = 2. Many children find the shopkeeper's method of counting on to find the difference rather than subtracting easier. This depends on the fact that addition and subtraction are inverses. Other important links for children to appreciate are that multiplication can be considered as repeated addition and similarly division as repeated subtraction. These connections help clarify these operations for children.

Number operation laws

There are three underlying laws which children will begin to discover from their work in the four operations and number patterns: the commutative, associative and distributive laws.

The *commutative law* applies to both addition and multiplication. This shows that the order in which the operation is performed does not alter the result:

a + b = b + a

a × b = b × a

These are true for all numbers a and b. Subtraction and division are not commutative because the order does matter. Children do sometimes make errors with subtraction and division because they try to apply the commutative law to them. It is important for children to recognise that 7 − 4 is not the same as 4 −7.

In Key Stage 1 children begin to appreciate this when learning their number bonds to 10 and spot that 7 + 3 = 10 and 3 + 7 = 10. Later, they will realise that the learning of the times tables is considerably simplified by this law. As more tables are learnt, there are fewer facts left to learn. By the time a child learns their four times table, they are usually already confident with 0, 1, 2, 3, 5 and 10 multiplied by 4, only leaving five new facts to learn.

> **TASK 4.1**
>
> *HLTA 2.2 Be familiar with the school curriculum, the age-related expectations of pupils, the main teaching methods and the testing/examination frameworks in the subjects and age ranges in which they are involved.*
>
> Can you work out how many different multiplication facts a child will learn in their primary school career, if learning their tables up to 10 × 10, including zeros? See Appendix 4 for possible answers.
>
> Tables are learned up to 10 × 10 rather than 12 × 12. This reflects the introduction of the decimal money system and metric measures. Children no longer need to calculate money with 240 pennies in a pound or 12 inches in a foot.

The *associative law* is closely linked to the commutative law. This too relates to the order in which an operation is to be performed. It shows that in the cases of addition and multiplication, if three or more elements are combined, the grouping and order do not affect the result:

$a + (b + c) = (a + b) + c$

$a \times (b \times c) = (a \times b) \times c$

These are true for all numbers a, b and c. Subtraction and division are not associative because the order does matter.

Many children seem to grasp this rule fairly intuitively, perhaps due to its close links to the commutative law. When adding three numbers, it doesn't matter where you start to add. For example, with 3 + 16 + 7, if you add 3 + 7 first for simplicity, it will not affect the sum.

The *distributive law* relates to multiplication and partitioning numbers through either addition or subtraction:

$a \times (b + c) = (a \times b) + (a \times c)$

$a \times (b - c) = (a \times b) - (a \times c)$

are true for all numbers a, b and c.

Multiplication is distributive over addition and subtraction. Division is not distributive.

An example of the distributive law in practice is the partitioning of large numbers in multiplication:

$3 \times 74 = 3 \times (70 + 4) = (3 \times 70) + (3 \times 4)$

This is an essential aspect of the informal grid method of multiplication and the standard algorithm for multiplication.

Addition

Counting forms the basis of addition. It is felt to be the most instinctive and straightforward to grasp and understand and so is usually the first of the four operations to be undertaken with children, with the use of concrete apparatus to aid their understanding.

There are two main types of addition:

- *Combining or aggregation.* This is where two quantities are placed together and then recounted as a single quantity. For example, Jane has three sweets and Peter has four. How many do they have altogether? The idea of how many or how much altogether is a central theme in this aspect of addition.
- *Augmentation.* This differs from the earlier type in that the original amount is increased in some way; it is augmented. For example, Jane has three sweets and Gran gives her three more; how many does she have now? These types of questions are often found in a shopping context, possibly involving an increase in price.

Associated with these concepts of addition is the notion of equivalence, where they begin to appreciate the idea that the 3 sweets and 4 sweets will equal 7 sweets. Addition often occurs in this comparison form.

The following case study shows young children using their counting skills to support their addition skills.

> **Case study 4.1 Kerry Hugill: Counting**
>
> I used Compare Bears of different colours and sizes with a group of four children, all aged three, to explore addition. I set up the bears by having two different colours (red and yellow). I picked three bears which were red and two bears which were yellow and asked the children how many bears there were. Two of the children went along the line and just counted the bears and then gave me the answers. One of the other children counted the three bears and then added the other two bears on in their head and gave me their answer. The fourth child counted how many bears of each colour and then counted them up all together and gave his answer.
>
> I placed one bear on each square of a number line up to the number seven. I then asked the children how many bears they thought they would need to get to number 10. I had to point out to the children where number 10 was on the number line and then the children selected how many bears they needed. A number line can be a useful continuous model for the teaching and learning of addition. For this part of the activity there was only one child who selected the right amount of bears. The other children had either selected too many bears or not enough.
>
> Next I put out all different coloured bears of all different sizes in no particular order. I asked, 'How can we arrange the teddies to make them easier to count?' This was a very interesting question as there was no correct answer – it was whatever was easiest for the child. There were quite a

few different outcomes to this activity. Some of the children grouped all the colours and others grouped similar sizes. Another method was they had all the colours mixed up but they put a big one then a little one all in a line and then counted them.

For the last activity I asked the children to add all of the different coloured bears together and all of the different sizes. I thought this would be a little hard for them but I was shocked to find that all of the children were able to pick out all of the different colours and all of the different sizes and give me a correct answer.

Subtraction

Subtraction is less intuitive than addition and is a more difficult concept for many children to grasp. There are three different meanings of subtraction which occur in the primary school curriculum which are all closely linked to addition and each other.

- *Reducing a quantity*. This is the earliest experience children will have of subtraction. A number can physically be reduced and children can separate the number into the number to be subtracted and the difference. Sometimes it is necessary to remove the objects completely for children to grasp the idea of 'taken away'. Jane has nine sweets and eats three, so how many does she have left?
- *Splitting or partitioning a quantity*. This is the type of understanding which is most commonly understood as subtraction. It is where a number is separated into two groups and is often related to how many or how much are left. This type of subtraction can be undertaken practically with objects, concretely with pictures and finally as part of more formal number operations.
- *Comparison of quantities*. This is often performed as a matching exercise to see which objects can be paired and thus to identify the difference, as in Figure 4.4. This leads to questions which can be phrased as: Jane has three sweets and Peter has five; how many more does Peter have?

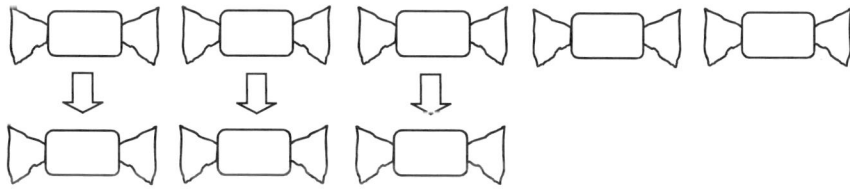

Figure 4.4 Comparison of quantities.

The language of subtraction does pose difficulties in the primary school. The result of a subtraction is called the difference. For instance, 'What is the difference between three and ten?' may result in answers such as 'ten is bigger than three' or 'three is odd and ten is even'. The emphasis on the careful and consistent use of mathematical vocabulary from an early age will help to address this, as discussed in Chapter 2.

Multiplication

Multiplication is usually introduced once children have a reasonably strong grasp of addition and subtraction. Certainly addition is a prerequisite skill. Multiplication can take a variety of forms including the following:

- *Equivalent groupings* (e.g. four groups of six children). This can be thought of as repeated aggregation or addition. It includes the early idea of multiplication phrased as 'lots of' and 'sets of'. This is often the type of multiplication children encounter first as it is a logical progression from addition. It can be conducted using practical apparatus, for example fingers, cubes or compare bears.
- *Rectangular array*. This represents the product in rows and columns, e.g. two rows and four columns as in Figure 4.5. It is a logical development from the equivalent groupings and illustrates the commutative law which is discussed earlier in this chapter.

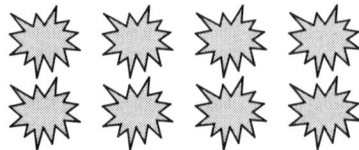

Figure 4.5 Rectangular array.

- *Scale factor (or enlargement)*. This refers to increasing at a steady rate. For example, if Jane has four sweets and Peter has three times as many, how many does Peter have? Function machines (see Figure 4.6) are also used to demonstrate scale factors.

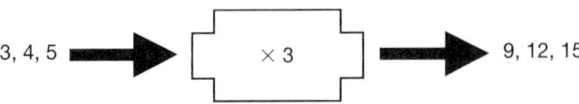

Figure 4.6 Function machine.

- *Rate*. This is linked to the concept of ratio. It has many real-life contexts which the children may already be familiar with, for instance shopping or being paid at an hourly rate. If one orange costs 23p, finding the cost of more than one orange would use this model of multiplication.

Scale factor and rate are introduced later in the primary school, once a sound understanding of the equivalent groups and confidence in the multiplication tables have been established.

Division

Multiplication and division are often taught in conjunction with each other, as the links between the two operations are very strong, being inverse operations. This knowledge underpins the understanding of division and it is almost impossible to divide without this fundamental understanding of multiplication.

Equal sharing is usually the first way a child will begin to divide, building on early experiences of sharing food or sweets. This is often undertaken using objects so the process and resulting groups can be seen. An example of this may be: nine sweets are shared among three children, so how many sweets will each child get? The first stages of this process begin with the 'one for me, one for you' type of sharing until the objects are used up.

A development of the sharing process is *equal grouping*; for example, how many bags of three sweets can be made from nine sweets? This again can be done practically with objects by counting out groups of three or by circling groups of pictures. At later stages multiplication tables are used to support this type of division.

Repeated subtraction is another way of viewing division. This is used when considering larger numbers and is part of the chunking process, an informal method of early long division where the numbers are too large to rely on multiplication knowledge. This is related to equal grouping described above.

Consider the question 137 divided by 6. The process involves subtracting multiples of the divisor, in this case 6. Chunking (see Figure 4.7) relies on using your prior knowledge of multiplication, selecting a multiple which you are confident of and subtracting this from the divisor. Ten times the divisor is often a straightforward place to start. In this way the size of the number is reduced to a manageable size and the knowledge of multiplication can be used to find 17 divided by 6 gradually. The 'chunks of 6' are then counted to show 22 lots of 6 remainder 5.

$$
\begin{array}{rl}
137 & \\
-60 & \quad 10 \times 6 \\
\hline
77 & \\
-60 & \quad 10 \times 6 \\
\hline
17 & \\
-12 & \quad 2 \times 6 \\
\hline
5 & \quad 22 \times 6 \\
\end{array}
$$

Figure 4.7 Chunking.

Case study 4.2 Tamsin Nash: Multiplication and division

The Year 6 numeracy group I work with everyday do seem to enjoy a challenge. Therefore a quiz seemed the best way to motivate them to answer my questions. I named the quiz 'How do you know that?' to remind the children that they were required to write down their methods of calculation as well as the answer.

12. How many methods can you use to find the answer to 2184 ÷ 14?

Question 12 showed the children's least favourite of the four operations giving them difficulties. This was a challenging question for Year 6 children as I used a four-digit number when they have mostly been used to three, even though the methods used should have been the same. The majority of the class showed two methods of answering this question, the least favourite being the column method, often with mistakes being made in the basic calculations. The most popular technique was the chunking method, which on the whole produced good results but surprisingly still showed errors in the simple subtraction operation needed.

However, the recurring mistake, when faced with a four-digit number being divided by a two-digit number was a misuse of partitioning. A number of the children showed their method of dealing with this question was to divide the large number 2184 first by 10 and then by 4, thinking that this would be a total division of 2184 by 14, when in fact it was by 40.

When asked the questions, 'How many ways can you find the answer to 21 × 99?' and 'Which did you find easiest?' I was surprised to see how many children chose the grid method. Although I feel most of the children use this technique for many two-digit multiplication questions, I felt more children would use the rounding method and either round the 21 down to 20 and add 99 or alternatively round the 99 up to 100 and take away 21. However, when thinking about this, I felt the children possibly used the method with the least room for error. The rounding method can lead to mistakes when deciding which of the two numbers must be either added or taken away after the easy multiplication part of the calculation has been completed.

I enjoyed looking through the all of the answers and their methods to see how they went about answering my questions. I found this offered a great insight as to their understanding of the teaching and I could see how easy it is to misunderstand when and how different methods should or could be used. While it is good for the children to be taught these different techniques to enable them to choose which one is best for their individual understanding, repeated discussion and explanation must occur and care must be taken not to move from one method to another too fast and risk leaving the children with a confused idea of which method belongs to which problem.

> **TASK 4.2**
>
> HLTA 2.3 Understand the aims, content, teaching strategies and intended outcomes for the lessons in which they are involved, and understand the place of these in the related teaching programme.
>
> Consider your own methods for solving these questions. Reflect on previous work with children in Key Stage 2 and consider the methods used and any misconceptions you encountered.

Fractions, decimals, percentages, ratio and proportion

Fractions, decimals and percentages are closely linked to an understanding of multiplication and division. Many children will have experienced some use of fractions at home in the sharing of food. Fractions in the Foundation Stage are generally in the context of measurement, for example half full and half empty, or within sharing activities. Real-life opportunities are used to reinforce an understanding of halves and quarters. It is important to emphasise the need for accurate use of vocabulary to avoid confusion. There is sometimes a more informal use of fractional parts, for instance a request for 'the bigger half' can be misleading showing that a child has not appreciated that halves should be of equal size.

Fractions are a notoriously difficult area of mathematics for children to grasp. Initially fractions are encountered as part of a unit or a whole. This is usually a shape, e.g. a circle, possibly a pizza or a cake, or a rectangle, often a bar of chocolate. Before the introduction of fractions each number consistently represents the same quantity, which is different from other numbers. However, when fractions are introduced, these numbers adopt a less straightforward identity. Now equivalent fractions provide examples which are equal, e.g. $\frac{2}{4} = \frac{3}{6}$. Also, the magnitude of the numbers is now counterintuitive; the larger the denominator, the smaller the fraction is also a common area of confusion.

Including fractions as part of a real-life problem-solving exercise will give the children chance to experience fractions in an accessible way and avoids reinforcing any misconceptions a more formal approach might have perpetuated.

> **Case study 4.3 Jacqui Johnson: Fractions and problem-solving**
>
> As part of a recent literacy lesson on following instructions, I made pizza with a group of ten Year 1 children. We returned to the classroom to share our pizza with the rest of the class. The problem: How could we share the pizzas equally between the 27 children in the class, the class teacher, head teacher and myself?
>
> I discussed this with the children. We had ten pizzas to share between 30 people. How could we make that easier to work out? We could cut one pizza into 30 pieces was a suggestion. But what about the other nine pizzas? Would it be sensible to cut each pizza into 30 pieces? If we did,

> how big would the pieces be? We agreed that the pieces would be tiny and that we would then have to cut the other nine pizzas into 30 pieces each to make it fair.
>
> We knew that ten pizzas were not enough for everyone so we drew ten circles on whiteboards and imagined that they were our pizzas. We drew a line down the middle to cut them in half. How many halves did we have? 20 – still not enough for everyone. What could we try next, I asked? Cut them again, the children suggested, so we dissected the imaginary pizzas into quarters. How many pieces do we have now? Let's count. 40 – too many.
>
> What can we do to get the right number of pieces? Talk to your partner for one minute and see if you can come up with a solution. After a few tries one child said to cut each pizza into three pieces which we did. I then asked the child, what makes you think that that will give us the right number of pieces? How did you get there? He answered that cutting the pizzas in half was not enough and cutting them into four gave us too many so it had to be three. I praised him for his logic and asked him to cut the pizzas into three equal pieces (as best he could) and hand them to everyone to see if he was correct in his prediction.
>
> While he was cutting the pizzas, with assistance, as a group we talked about sharing things out and that maths and numbers really help us. We don't just need numbers in the classroom but everyday, in all sorts of situations, from Pizza Hut to deciding how many cream buns to buy for tea when granny and grandpa come to visit.
>
> I do not feel that getting the right number of slices was the most important part of this exercise, but the process of thought to get there. It would have been far easier to just chop them up and hand them out but our discussion during the actual cooking set the scene for sharing equally. Although the word 'fractions' was not mentioned in the session we did talk about halves, quarters and eventually thirds.

Fractions are related to decimals, percentages, proportion and ratio. The examples below are adapted from the Primary National Numeracy Strategy.

There are 24 children in the class and 6 of them are boys.
- As a fraction – one quarter $\frac{1}{4}$ of the children in the class are boys.
- As a decimal – 0.25 of the children in the class are boys.
- As a percentage – 25 per cent of the children in the class are boys.
- As a proportion – one in every four of the children in the class is a boy.
- As a ratio – the ratio of boys to girls in the class is 1 to 3 or 1 : 3, or there is one boy for every three girls.

TASK 4.3

HLTA 2.1 Have sufficient understanding of your specialist area to support pupils' learning, and be able to acquire further knowledge to contribute effectively and with confidence to the classes in which you are involved.

Ratio and proportion are often confused. Try to explain the difference between ratio and proportion in your own words.

In a class of 28 children there are 16 boys and 12 girls.

Write this as a ratio and as a proportion.

If two more boys join the class, how does this affect the ratio of girls and boys and the proportion of each within the class?

Key Points

- Counting is an essential prerequisite skill for the understanding of number and is comprised of several elements.
- A good understanding of the underlying principles and the links between the four operations is necessary in order to support the learning of number effectively.
- Learners (young and older) find the understanding of fractions significantly more difficult than other common mathematical concepts.

Reflections

Do you understand the relationships between different operations?

Do you understand the methods you use?

Shape, space and measures

> This chapter will help you to:
>
> - consolidate your knowledge of the language of shape and space
> - understand progression in measures
> - develop a wide range of activities to use with children

Shape and space include the properties of 3D and 2D shapes, symmetry, position and direction, and movement and angle. Measures include the measurement of length, mass, capacity, area and time. They are grouped together as attainment target Ma3 in the National Curriculum; in the Primary Framework for mathematics the corresponding strands are Understanding Shape and Measuring.

Shape and space

Work with children in this area must be practical. The skill of the adult lies in providing a wide range of activities, not just relying on a few, and in knowing and using correct and precise mathematical language.

The language of shape to which children are introduced is commonly that of the 2D or 'flat' shapes: square, circle, triangle and the notorious oblong, of which more later. However, the young child's first experience of manipulating shapes is much more likely to be with 'solid' 3D shapes in the form of brightly coloured building bricks, or tins and boxes from the shops, so they should also be introduced to words such as cuboid and cylinder.

Young children come into school with experience of shape and space through interacting with their environment. However, as discussed in Chapter 2, they are likely to use everyday language rather than the more precise mathematical language. For example, both a circle and a sphere may be described as 'the round shape'. 'Bigger' might describe height, weight or thickness. Children are not the only users of imprecise language. What is a child to make of the adult's request to 'Give me the square brick'? It is important to build up correct vocabulary. There is little point in learning one name for a shape, only to be told at a later date that it is really called something else. Instead use correct mathematical language alongside the more familiar language from the start.

> **TASK 5.1**
>
> *HLTA 3.1.2 Working within a framework set by the teacher, plan your role in lessons including how to provide feedback to pupils.*
>
> For your next mathematics session involving shape, check your own understanding of the terms you will need. Prepare in advance the definitions and explanations you will give to the children.

2D and 3D shapes

Polygons are closed plane (flat, two-dimensional) shapes with straight sides. Polyhedra (singular polyhedron; polyhedrons is an allowed plural) are three-dimensional shapes with flat faces that are polygons. They are often called solid shapes, but they can be hollow, and they can be frameworks made of wire or straws. The word regular has a special meaning when referring to shapes. Regular polygons have all their sides and all their angles equal, otherwise they are called irregular. Regular polyhedra have all their faces identical. See Figure 5.1 for more vocabulary.

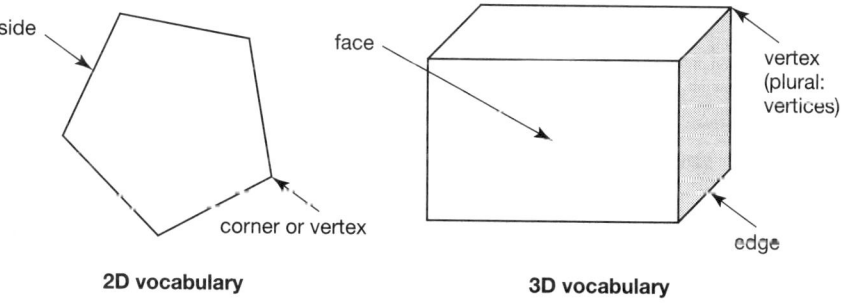

2D vocabulary   3D vocabulary

Figure 5.1 Shape vocabulary.

The names of polygons come from the number of sides. Children often find it helpful to have the prefixes explained and related to more familiar objects; tri means three, as in tricycle, while a quad-bike has four wheels. Your school may be built round a quadrangle. An octopus has eight legs. A decade has ten years.

Among the curved shapes, a circle is a shape in which every point on the circumference is the same distance from the centre. If the shape is flattened, it is an ellipse; a curved shape is only an oval if one end is fatter than the other (like an egg, but 2D).

It is very important that children have lots of experience of irregular as well as regular shapes; can they recognise that a four-pointed star is an octagon? Equally important is ensuring children recognise shapes in different orientations; a square standing on one corner is not transformed into a diamond, it is still a square.

> **TASK 5.2**
>
> HLTA 3.1.3 Contribute effectively to the selection and preparation of teaching resources that meet the diversity of pupils' needs and interests.
>
> Think about how you show shapes to children. Do you always show them in the same orientation? Do you always show the same kind? Are your triangles always equilateral? Do you ever show very long, thin oblongs? Think of ways in which you can enrich children's experience of shape. See Appendix 5 for some suggestions.

Classifying shapes

Sorting and classifying shapes by different criteria is an excellent way of helping children to identify the precise properties of the wide variety of shapes available.

- A *quadrilateral* is any plane shape with four straight sides (see Figure 5.2).

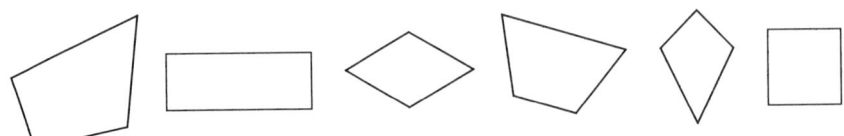

Figure 5.2 Various quadrilaterals.

- If only one pair of sides is parallel, it is a *trapezium*. Figure 5.3 is an isosceles trapezium because the two non-parallel sides are the same length.

Figure 5.3 Trapezium.

- If both pairs of opposite sides are parallel (always the same distance apart) it is a *parallelogram*, as in Figure 5.4.

Figure 5.4 Parallelogram.

- If the parallelogram has four right angles (all its corners are 90°) it is a *rectangle*, as in Figure 5.5.

Figure 5.5 Different rectangles.

This is a good time to consider the four-sided shape which has four right angles but is not a square because its length and breadth are different. Is it an oblong or a rectangle? The definition of a rectangle is a quadrilateral with four right angles; its opposite sides are equal and parallel. Thus a square is a special rectangle, one in which all four sides are of equal length. If the length and breadth are not equal, then the rectangle is called an oblong. So, squares and oblongs are both rectangles; the set of squares and the set of oblongs are sub-sets of the set of rectangles. The set of rectangles is itself a sub-set of the set of parallelograms, which is in turn a sub-set of the set of quadrilaterals; the set of quadrilaterals is a sub-set of the set of polygons.

> **TASK 5.3**
>
> HLTA 3.2.2 Monitor pupils' responses to learning tasks and modify their approach accordingly.
>
> How do children show you shapes? Do they always draw them on paper or whiteboards, or do they use geoboards and elastic bands, or their fingers? Think about different ways in which your pupils could demonstrate their understanding of the properties of shapes. It is vital that children, when showing you a triangle, for instance, recognise that they need a shape which has three straight sides and three angles. The length of the sides and the size of the angles are not important unless they are asked to show a particular type of triangle.

A long piece of elastic, 5 or 6 metres, sewn or knotted to make a loop, can be used to experiment with making 2D shapes. Children stand inside the loop and lift it up so that the elastic rests on their ankles. By moving, they stretch the elastic to make shapes. The adult can give instructions, 'Can you make a square? What shapes can you make?' The rest of the class can be questioned by the adult or can offer advice or instructions to the children in the elastic.

Maths trails – walks on which children solve mathematical questions either in school or outside – are an excellent way of giving pupils practical experience in a different context. Shapes in particular lend themselves to a maths trail for young children. It is very important that children realise that shapes are not just those brightly coloured plastic objects in the classroom but can be found all around them. Children need to recognise not the object but the shape, to generalise and to recognise, for example, the 'squareness' of a square. Maths trails allow adult and child to break away from the familiar neat commercial apparatus and limited range of examples.

> **Case study 5.1 Tamsin Nash: Maths trail**
>
> Once outside the children were immediately faced with squares and rectangles from the exterior of the building. After a few directions from me the children began to see trapeziums, parallelograms and irregular quadrilaterals in the environment around them. The children worked well together, pointing out shapes to each other and this led to some great discussion with comments such as one on the three different quadrilaterals on the picnic table: a rectangle, a square and 'a brilliant' trapezium.
>
> The children really enjoyed this quest, and through their discussions I was aware of their thinking about the properties they needed to find the quadrilaterals; for example, there was a discussion as to whether the brickwork was a parallelogram as it had two pairs of parallel lines or a rectangle because opposite sides were equal. The children themselves came up with the solution that some of these shapes could go on both sheets. This was also found to be the case for the rhombus. As we got towards the end of the trail the rhombus worksheet only had two entries. I suggested we looked at some squares and discussed the properties we were looking for, thus revealing that a square is actually a special rhombus. The group decided this was something new and couldn't wait to tell the teacher!

The National Numeracy Strategy recommends visualisation activities as another way of developing shape understanding.

TASK 5.4

HLTA 1.6 Be able to improve your own practice, including through observation, evaluation and discussion with colleagues.

Try this activity with a colleague.

Imagine a square (all four sides the same length, all angles 90°).

Now imagine a second square, the same size as the first, next to the first so that they share a side (no overlap).

What shape do you have now? Does it matter where you put the second square?

Bring on a third square the same size so that it shares a common side with one of the others.

What shape do you have now? Does it matter where you put it?

Now imagine a fourth square the same size as the others and join it to one of the sides of your shape.

What shape do you have now? Were any other shapes possible at any stage? (See Appendix 5 for possible arrangements.)

Did you and your colleague have the same shapes all the way through? Did you find this activity easy or difficult?

Polyhedra often take their names from the number of their faces, though some have their own, more familiar, names; thus a solid shape with six faces is a hexahedron, but if all its faces are squares it is a cube. There are five polyhedra which can be regular: the tetrahedron or triangle-based pyramid (four faces); the hexahedron or cube (six faces); the octahedron (eight faces); the dodecahedron (twelve faces); and the icosahedron (20 faces). Most 3D shapes children encounter are irregular; a cereal box is a cuboid because although all the corners of the faces are right angles, the faces themselves are oblongs. Pyramids stand on a flat base, with the other, triangular, faces meeting at a point at the top (a common vertex). Prisms are solid shapes with a constant cross-section. The ends are identical and can be any polygon; the other faces are all rectangles. Many pencils, if they were not sharpened to a point, would be hexagonal prisms. Chocolates are packed in many interesting shapes, including cylinders, pyramids and triangular, hexagonal and octagonal prisms.

A 'feely bag' provides a good activity for helping children develop their understanding of 3D shapes. A collection of solid shapes is put into a cloth bag, then a child puts one hand inside and finds a shape. Keeping the shape hidden inside the bag, the child feels it and describes it. The child can be asked to say what the shape is her/himself or other children can identify it from the description. The adult can help by supporting the use of correct language, 'What shape are the faces? Are all the faces the same shape?'

> **Case study 5.2 Lynn Pope: Shape vocabulary**
>
> We looked farther in the playground. 'We can't find anything square!' exclaimed L. I could see some toy building blocks, some cuboids and some cubes. I pointed to the cube asking, 'What can you tell me about this toy block?' giving L an open ended question that would encourage her to think about the shape and its properties. 'It's got square faces. (pause) It's a cube!' she announced with great delight. This highlighted the fact that L understood the properties of a cube and she used mathematical language to describe it. 'Well done L. Can you tell me how many square faces the cube has?' '1, 2, 3, 4, 5 … 6,' she answered. This helped me to identify that she understood that the shape was 3D and she could see and count the faces.
>
> I then asked her to find me a cuboid. 'What is the difference between the cuboid and the cube?' L answered, 'It's got two square faces and longer sides.' I explained that the faces with the longer sides had their own name, that a shape with four sides, two long and two short, was an oblong.

Children also need to construct 3D shapes. Do not rely simply on printed templates; construction apparatus can be used to build shapes, then carefully unfolded to demonstrate the outline (called the net) and then be transferred to squared card. When shapes are being designed and built, frequent reference should be made to the properties of the shape.

One problem of language arises from working with 2D shapes. By definition, a 2D shape has no thickness; we can draw a triangle on the board or project a square onto a screen without causing problems. However, even the thinnest paper has measurable thickness (if we have the correct measuring apparatus), so when the triangle is cut out it becomes a 3D shape. The commonly used flat plastic shapes are at least 0.5 mm thick. If a shape can be handled, it is a 3D shape; the correct use of mathematical language is compromised when we ask children to 'sort the collection of 2D shapes'. We need to be aware that the flat card or plastic shapes we ask children to work with are *representations* of 2D shapes, and when a child holds up a 'circle' and says 'this is a cylinder', he or she is right and needs congratulating not correcting.

It is possible to use cards with drawings of 2D shapes for children to sort. This allows children to work with 2D shapes without compromising the use of correct language. However, in practice most children can accept the compromise of using very thin objects to represent 2D shapes, as long as we know it is a compromise.

Children can use their 2D and 3D shapes to make patterns. In so doing, they will discover that some flat shapes will fit together without any spaces in between, while others do not. This fitting together is called *tessellation*, and finding shapes which tessellate is a good sorting activity; working out why they do so is a good investigation.

Movement

Shapes can be moved in three basic ways. They can be *translated*, i.e. moved from one position to another without changing orientation. They can be *reflected*, i.e. flipped over to produce a mirror image. They can be *rotated*, i.e. turned around some point which may be inside or outside the shape.

Children can recognise translations in repeating patterns such as in wallpaper, fabric or architectural design features, and can design their own. Card or plastic shapes, pinboards and elastic bands, pegs and pegboards, squared, dotted and plain paper can all be used to make patterns which can be repeated or copied as if they were reflected in an imaginary mirror. It is very helpful to have plastic mirrors to show children initially what they are aiming for. When constructing reflected images, it is important to experience different orientations of the mirror line (horizontal, vertical and diagonal), and towards the end of Key Stage 2 children need to know that objects are reflected on both sides of the mirror line.

Children will also need to look for lines of symmetry within shapes, e.g. by folding paper shapes in half. Shapes can be sorted according to the number of lines of symmetry they have.

Folded paper and thick paint are often used to make butterfly pictures. This is a good way to introduce ideas of reflection and symmetry, but we need to remember that the nature of the process means they will not get a perfect reflection when they press the paper onto the sticky paint. Children need to know that in reflective symmetry any feature on one side of the line of symmetry is mirrored on the other side.

Children can be given sheets of capital or upper case letters and asked to pick out those which are symmetrical. Make sure you choose your font carefully; there is a significant difference between an **Arial A** and a Times New Roman **A**.

These two activities are frequently used to explore reflective symmetry and there is a danger of them being repeated in successive years. Children need to be given the opportunity to create symmetrical patterns and diagrams, to investigate pictures and objects and explain, for example, why the classroom door or a human face is not exactly symmetrical.

Rotational symmetry is the property of a shape which allows it to be rotated and to look exactly the same. It is described in terms of orders. Every shape has an order of rotational symmetry of at least 1. This means that if it is turned round completely (rotated through 360°) it will fit back upon itself; you get back to where you started. A square has an order of 4 because every time you rotate it through 90° it fits on top of itself. An equilateral triangle has order 3; all regular polygons have an order of rotational symmetry that matches their number of sides.

Children will have experience of rotation through PE and playing with toys. When working on rotational symmetry they need opportunities to rotate shapes, on tracing paper or acetate. It is a good idea to mark one corner, to make the orientation of the shape clear as it rotates.

ICT is a very valuable resource when teaching about all aspects of shape and space. Drawing and painting packages allow shapes to be copied and moved from one place to another (translated), to be flipped (reflected) and to be rotated. These properties can be used not only to demonstrate mathematical ideas, but to show the links between maths, art and design and design technology. Digital cameras can be used to photograph shapes in the school grounds, or symmetrical shapes made in PE. These can then be projected on the whiteboard for demonstration and discussion. Interactive teaching programs (ITPs) referred to in Chapter 2 are also available to support several aspects of shape and space.

Eventually children should be able to recognise combinations of translation, reflection and rotation and be able to identify the individual transformations.

Describing position

When children are learning about rotation they should do this by turning themselves as well as objects, and recognise the term angle as a measure of turn. This can be done in PE as well as in mathematics, with children learning to turn clockwise and anticlockwise, that a quarter turn is one right angle and that a complete turn is four right angles. By learning where North, East, South and West are, each direction separated by a right angle, links with geography can be made clear. Later they can learn that a right angle is 90° and one complete turn is 360°.

Children start to learn about position through the use of positional language: above, below, beside, clockwise. It is important that the use of this language is identified in PE and geography as well as in mathematics. Numeracy across the curriculum should be very evident in shape, space and measures.

At Key Stage 1 children need to be able to move a counter on squared paper and describe its movement as, say, three squares along and one square up. Coordinates (sometimes referred to as Cartesian coordinates) are not introduced until Key Stage 2. The horizontal and vertical axes are drawn on squared paper, and where they meet is called the origin. The horizontal and vertical distances of a point from the origin are its coordinates. Children need to recognise that the point (5, 2) is different from the point (2, 5) (see Figure 5.6).

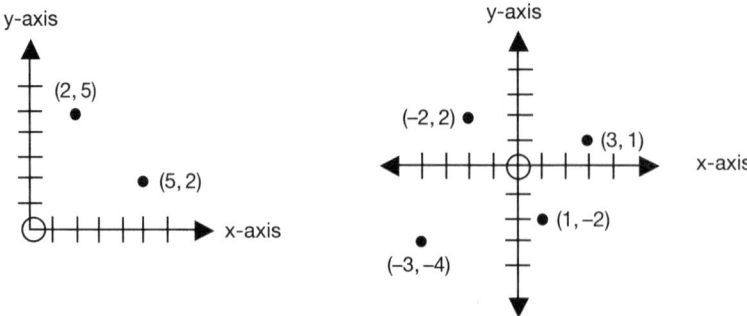

Figure 5.6 Coordinates.

There are obvious links with map work in geography, and coordinates also lend themselves to whole-class work with children as living examples. Set chairs out in a rectangular grid, number the columns and rows, and ask questions. The traditional paper and pencil game of 'battleships' is an entertaining way of using coordinates; if you are not happy with the military connotations of this, make it a television crew looking for rare animals in the jungle. Initially children work with coordinates in the first quadrant. By the end of Year 6 they should be able to describe coordinates in all four quadrants (see Figure 5.6).

> **TASK 5.5**
>
> *HLTA 3.2.2 Monitor pupils' responses to learning tasks and modify their approach accordingly.*
>
> How would you describe your location at this moment? How many different ways can you find to describe it? Ask some children in the classroom to describe their position. Can you encourage them to think of different ways? See Appendix 5 for some suggestions.

Research summary – The Van Hiele model of geometric thought

During the 1950s two Dutch educators, Pierre and Dina Van Hiele, suggested a sequenced structure for the way children develop their mathematical thinking in geometry. They described five levels of thought through which children must progress in sequence. Since then these Van Hiele levels have been the subject of further research (Burger and Shaughnessy, 1986) and are described here for you to consider when working with your pupils. In some literature the levels are numbered 1–5, though the Van Hieles used 0–4. Movement from one level to the next is not related to age, but to mathematical experiences.

- *Level 0 (Visualisation)*. Children recognise shapes by appearance, not properties, so, for example, a child may happily recognise a 'conventional' equilateral triangle but not a scalene triangle.
- *Level 1 (Analysis)*. Children recognise shapes by their properties. They can describe various properties of a shape, though they often cannot distinguish which are the most important, identifying, properties. They know that size and orientation are not important in identifying a shape.
- *Level 2 (Abstraction or Informal Deduction)*. Children recognise the relationships between properties of shapes and can follow logical arguments about the properties. They can, for example, recognise that a square is a rectangle because it has the properties of a rectangle.
- *Level 3 (Deduction)* and *Level 4 (Rigor)*. These relate to the ability to construct and understand geometric proofs and are not normally applicable at primary school level.

The Van Hiele theory suggests that children need to have a wide range of geometric experience to move from one level to the next, and that teaching pitched at a level higher than that of the child may make understanding harder not easier.

Children's understanding of shape and space can be limited by the experiences they are given and the opportunities made available to them. They need as big a range as possible, including real objects as well as maths apparatus, outdoors as well as indoors, describing mental images, making and analysing shapes and explaining what they have done.

Measures

Children need lots of practical experience in estimating and comparing measures as well as learning the skills to use measuring instruments. This applies across the range of measures, and needs to be progressive, moving from comparing objects, through the use of non-standard units to the use of standard units. We start by comparing objects and developing vocabulary; the table is longer than the book; the jug holds more than the cup. We then introduce measurement by using physical units which children handle; the book is two bricks long. When children understand the concept of measuring with units, they can use measuring instruments; the book is 15 cm long.

To begin with, children should compare two objects directly, side by side, so they might hold a drinking straw and a crayon next to each other to see which is the longer. Encourage them to say not only 'the straw is longer than the crayon', but also 'the crayon is shorter than the straw'.

When considering mass and capacity young children often struggle with the concept of conservation, as noted by Piaget. If you take a lump of plasticene and change its shape many children will believe that the mass has changed as well. The fact that this can change the density so that now the plasticene floats causes further confusion. With capacity, young children often believe that a tall graduated cylinder holds more than a shallow dish, even when you pour the water from one to the other.

> **TASK 5.6**
>
> *HLTA 1.6 Be able to improve their own practice, including through observation, evaluation and discussion with colleagues.*
>
> When comparing the length of two objects, a common error is that the child does not line them up from the same baseline. Discuss with a colleague what problems there might be when children are comparing the weight of two objects or the capacity of two containers. Try observing children to see if you are right.

When children can confidently compare two objects, they can move on to comparing and ordering three or more objects. Correct language is again essential: the pencil is the lightest; the brick is the heaviest; the box is heavier than the pencil but lighter than the brick.

Children can make a line of toys which is the same length as the table, or see how many different containers they can fill from a jug. The next step is to bring about some uniformity by using several copies of the same toy or container, then use one item repeatedly. Children could line up the number of egg cups it takes to fill a mug then progress to using one egg cup repeatedly and counting.

When children are confident using non-standard units, they can be directed to some of the difficulties, if they have not already found them for themselves. Measuring using strides and choosing the shortest and the tallest pupils to find the length of the classroom will give two different results which are both correct. This can lead to a discussion of how to avoid confusion; children will usually come up with the idea of everyone using the same thing to measure length. When introduced to standard metric units, children need to develop a feel for the size of each unit, using it as a benchmark to estimate.

> **TASK 5.7**
>
> *HLTA 1.6 Be able to improve your own practice, including through observation, evaluation and discussion with colleagues.*
>
> What are the standard units for these aspects of measures: length, capacity, weight, time, temperature? Find items which can serve as benchmarks for each of these units. What sort of clothes would you wear for 0°C, 10°C, 20°C and 30°C? See Appendix 5 for suggestions.

Once children are using standard measures they will be using measuring instruments, such as rulers and thermometers, so they need to be able to read the scale. There are two key things they need to know: to start their measurement from zero and how much each division is worth. It is a good idea to give children experience of a range of scales, drawing them on the board and working out what each division represents. The ITP which demonstrates a measuring cylinder has already been mentioned in Chapter 2; other ITPs also support work on measures.

In all forms of measurement, children should be encouraged to estimate first. They can be very reluctant to do this, but given a classroom atmosphere where all contributions are valued, lots of practice should develop the skill.

Children sometimes confuse perimeter and area. Perimeter is the distance all the way round the boundary of a shape. Area is a measure of the surface enclosed by the boundary. Children start by covering, say, a table with leaves or books or similar objects and counting how many are needed. They recognise the need to cover the surface completely, linking this to tessellation. They are then introduced to standard units, which for area are square units, in upper Key Stage 2.

Children can think that there is a link between perimeter and area when there is not. Shapes with the same perimeter do not have to have the same area, as a range of examples drawn on squared paper will show.

> **Case study 5.3 Tamsin Nash: Perimeter and area**
>
> We began the investigation with a discussion on the possible outcomes. The children were asked if making the area of a shape bigger would also make the perimeter bigger and all six answered no. The children went on to talk of different shapes having an effect, so I asked what shape they thought would make a difference. They disagreed on the answer. Some suggested any shape provided it was tall and thin and others felt that the more sides the shape had, the larger the perimeter. The children themselves felt that, to keep the investigation simple, they should start with rectangles with different areas, then expand to rectangles with the same area but different length and width. They also elected to change the shape slightly and use an 'L' shape (made of two rectangles to keep calculations simple) and a 'U' shape (three rectangles). They then settled down to their first task, making rectangles with a bigger area each time and measuring the perimeter.
>
> After completing this stage the children's hypothesis was:
>
> The area goes up in 4s while the perimeter goes up in 2s.
> For example, when A = 12, P = 14; when A = 16, P = 16; when A = 20, P = 18.
>
> I asked the children if this answered our original question: when the area gets bigger does the perimeter get bigger too? They decided the answer was yes, but at a different rate. The group then went on to the second phase of their investigation, keeping the area the same and changing the length and width of the rectangle. This was a great experiment as the children soon saw that they could make the perimeter change significantly without changing the area. One child used half squares, which raised the question from another as to how could they keep the same area if the width measurement was only $\frac{1}{2}$, as multiplying by half is the same as dividing by 2. The first stressed that this was the whole point because she could then make the sides twice as long, giving a huge increase in perimeter.
>
> I felt this investigation was of great value because this group already had a good grasp of the facts relating area to perimeter and could use this knowledge to explore further and extend their predicting and application skills. One of the limitations of the task was that we only considered rectangles. Had I had more time and know-how it might have been possible to extend this task with an ICT resource.

The National Numeracy Strategy skips over volume in favour of capacity. Volume is the measurement of the amount of space an object takes up, and is measured in cubic centimetres (cm^3) or cubic metres (m^3). Capacity is the measurement of the amount a hollow object can hold, measured in millilitres (ml) or litres (l). Children gain experience of capacity through filling and emptying containers, often with water, though sand or rice can be used.

Children will often think that a tall, thin container will hold more than a short, fat one when in fact they hold the same amount. Lots of experience and discussion is needed, and much of this can take place during play. Structured play is an essential part of developing concepts in mathematics.

The distinction between weight and mass can be a problem, though perhaps more for adults than young children. Mass, a term more common in science than in everyday speech, is a measure in grams and kilograms of how much matter there is in an object. Weight in scientific terms is a measure of the force exerted on an object by gravity and is measured in Newtons. You would weigh less on the Moon than you do on the Earth because the gravity is less, but your mass would remain the same. Rather than say, for example, that a shoe *weighs* 500 g, it is better to say it *has a mass of* 500 g. However, the National Curriculum (DfEE, 1999) says it is acceptable to treat weight as synonymous with mass at Key Stage 1. At Key Stage 2 the term Newton can be introduced. This is an area where correct mathematical language is strongly at variance with common usage.

As with so much work on measures, children need a lot of practical experience, comparing the weight of objects, balancing them and reading scales. This cannot be a paper exercise; the child must be actively engaged and encouraged to talk about what they are doing.

Many children seem to find time difficult. This is not surprising, as it involves two separate activities. One is reading either an analogue dial or a digital display to tell the time, the other is measuring the passage of time. As adults we know that the apparent passage of time can seem very different depending on what we are doing. Children can use sand timers to experience the passing of 1, 2 or 5 minutes, and can be helped to establish a rhythm for counting seconds. Telling the time is a complex process, requiring as it does the reading of a circular scale and two (or three) hands that move at different rates. Added to that are the different ways we say the time (eight thirty-five, twenty-five to nine). The adult needs to make sure that the child has a correct understanding of all these aspects; there are many opportunities for confusion.

When the Cockcroft Report was published in 1982, primary school children were already being taught metric units of measurement. However, Britain has still not converted to full metrication, and many of us are still more familiar with imperial measures. As adults working in education, we need to be personally familiar with the concepts we are teaching, but we may find it easier to visualise an inch or a foot rather than a centimetre or a metre.

TASK 5.8

HLTA 1.3 Demonstrate and promote the positive values, attitudes and behaviour you expect from the pupils with whom you work.

Do you know your own height and weight in metric units? If not, go now and measure your height in metres and your weight in kilograms and memorise the information.

Shape, space and measures are enjoyable aspects of mathematics for children and are frequently used in subjects such as science, geography and design technology. One of the tasks of the adult is to help children develop their understanding of the mathematics and draw attention to its importance across the curriculum and life.

> **Key Points**
> - Work on shape, space and measures must be practical and include a wide range of experiences.
> - Knowing and using correct vocabulary is essential; incorrect language leads to misconceptions.
> - Cross-curricular links strengthen children's understanding of shape, space and measures.

> **Reflections**
>
> Are you confident with the large number of definitions used in shape, space and measures?
>
> Do you regularly and systematically use correct vocabulary?
>
> Do you draw children's attention to aspects of space shape and measures when they are used in subjects other than mathematics?

Data handling

> This chapter will help you to:
>
> - consolidate your knowledge of a variety of forms of data handling
> - utilise the whole data cycle
> - recognise and address some common difficulties children encounter in data handling

Data handling in the National Curriculum and NNS includes several different areas: sorting and matching; collecting, processing and interpreting data; statistics and probability. Although data handling as a separate attainment target (Ma4) begins at Key Stage 2, it exists in Key Stage 1 hidden at the end of Number (Ma2) and integrated into the Curriculum Guidance for the Foundation Stage (CGFS). Many children will have experienced the basis of data handling, sorting and matching, at home in everyday activities such as matching socks and setting the table and in games such as pairs. This is developed during the Foundation Stage.

The phrase 'lies, damn lies and statistics', attributed to Benjamin Disraeli, is probably more true today than it was in Victorian times. We are bombarded with data in many forms through the media, daily work and leisure but many people lack confidence in interpreting this data. This insecurity might be due to the use of data by the media and government to influence our views. This makes it especially important that children are taught to understand data.

Research summary – Teachers' confidence in data handling

A small-scale research study by Price and Raiker (1999) revealed that the sample teachers lacked confidence in data handling and found teaching it difficult. One factor that the researchers noted was that over-reliance on published mathematics schemes further reduced teacher confidence and lowered pupil achievement. Although this was especially true of the teachers in the sample, it was generally true of all of the staff and as a result INSET on data handling was provided. A questionnaire after the INSET sessions showed that teachers' confidence had increased greatly and results for Year 4 optional SATs improved significantly from the previous year in both schools. Observations of the lessons after the INSET showed a greater range of questioning, including open questions, which resulted in the children developing a deeper understanding rather than merely answering superficial questions.

Since this study demonstrated that training in data handling was beneficial to teaching, this chapter combines knowledge about data handling with knowledge about how to teach it. Although most adults are familiar with graphs and tables, the different systems used for sorting are less familiar.

Sorting

The criteria for sorting often include size, colour and shape, though other attributes can be used; deciding on one is harder than you might think. In order to choose how to sort you need to survey the collection of objects, recognise what they have in common and how they differ and then decide which of these aspects occur frequently enough to divide the collection into reasonable piles. This is quite a complex process so most young children find it too difficult to select suitable criteria. To develop the children's skills encourage them to discuss the similarities and differences of the collection. Then use these to suggest several possible criteria for sorting and get the children to choose which to use. High-attaining children could be encouraged to select their own and explain why some criteria are more useful than others for sorting a given set of objects.

TASK 6.1

HLTA 1.6 Be able to improve their own practice, including through observation, evaluation and discussion with colleagues.

With a partner, find a handful of mixed coins. How many different ways can you sort them? What sort of attributes were you using? Did you sort into two piles or several or a different number each time?

Now make a collection of 12 random objects. Can you find a way to split them into roughly equal groups? How many ways could you sort them? How did you decide on your criteria? Discuss your findings together. Then plan what you would ask children to help them think about those criteria.

There are several diagrams that can help with sorting. Venn and Carroll diagrams were the result of a mathematical battle between John Venn and Charles Dodgson (better known as Lewis Carroll) in the late 1800s.

Venn diagrams use circles for sorting. Most schools have hinged plastic hoops for this purpose. An object is either inside the circle if it matches the criterion, or outside the circle if it does not (see Figure 6.1). It can help to have the circle on a large piece of paper so there is a clearly defined area showing objects outside the circle as opposed to those that are still waiting to be sorted.

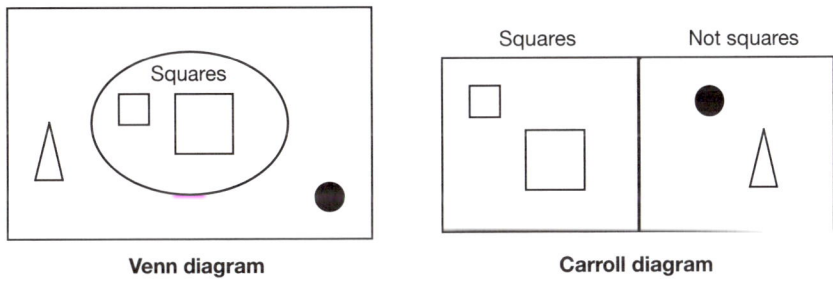

Figure 6.1 Single-criterion Venn and Carroll diagrams.

Carroll diagrams contain all objects within boxes. These are labelled 'criteria' and 'not criteria' (see Figure 6.1). For example, numbers may be labelled even and not even. This is not always done properly in schools or in textbooks, where such a set may be labelled even and odd. This may seem like a minor point but the importance of correct labels becomes more apparent when it says 'squares' and 'triangles' instead of 'squares' and 'not squares'. What would happen in that case if you had a shape that was neither a square nor a triangle?

The previous examples showed sorting by a single criterion, which is the simplest level. Primary school children also learn how to sort using two criteria. With Venn diagrams this involves two overlapping circles with four areas for sorting. Where the two circles overlap is called the intersection and means that the object must meet the criteria of both circles. Children often have difficulty understanding what objects can go in the intersection and sometimes put things in there that do not meet either criteria, in other words things that should be excluded from both circles.

Children can have trouble selecting two criteria that relate to different attributes of the object. This is where Carroll diagrams can be clearer with their criterion/not criterion test (see Figure 6.2). A good test is to see if you can find examples for all sections of the diagram.

68 SUPPORTING NUMERACY

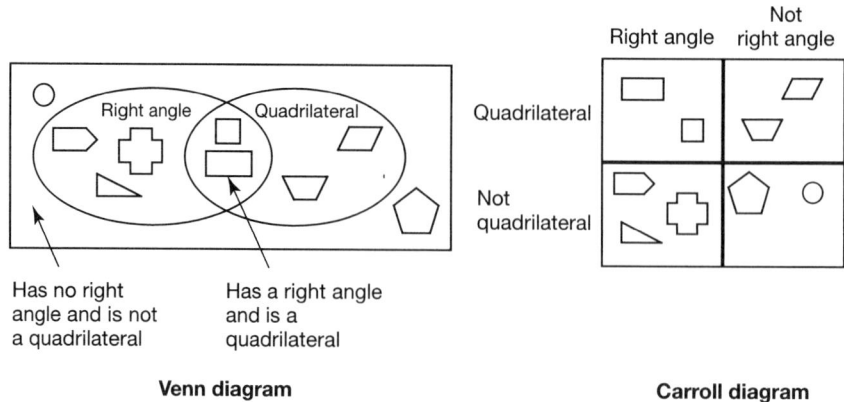

Venn diagram   **Carroll diagram**

Figure 6.2 Two-criteria Venn and Carroll diagrams.

TASK 6.2

HLTA 3.1.3 Contribute effectively to the selection and preparation of teaching resources that meet the diversity of pupils' needs and interests.

Think of two criteria that would sort the following numbers using Venn and Carroll diagrams: {1, 2, 3, 4, 5, 6, 7, 8, 9, 10}. How can diagrams like these be used in your setting?

Venn and Carroll diagrams can also be used with three criteria (see Figure 6.3), although Venn diagrams are more commonly used in schools. These are used for sorting in science lessons, as well as in mathematics lessons.

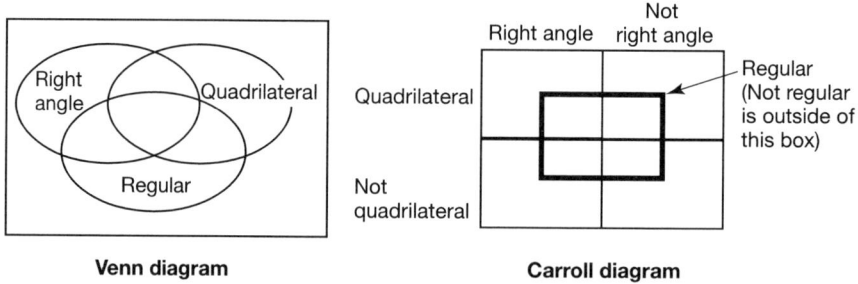

Venn diagram   **Carroll diagram**

Figure 6.3 Three-criteria Venn and Carroll diagrams.

The logical thinking involved in using Venn or Carroll diagrams provides a good extension for high-attaining children. A real challenge for older children is to design Venn and Carroll diagrams for four criteria. How many sections would there be?

Branch diagrams (also known as tree diagrams and decision trees) are another way of sorting items. They differ from Venn and Carroll diagrams in that you usually keep sorting until each item has its individual destination. At each branch there is a yes/no question. There is a children's game where you have to ask questions in order to identify the mystery person. After each question the people who don't match the answer are turned down. More questions are asked until eventually there is only one person left. This is the same process used in a branch diagram. There are several computer programs for using and creating branch diagrams. In some, the diagram is already set up and the children use it to identify mystery objects. Others allow the children to create their own branch diagrams.

The data cycle

Another aspect of data handling is collecting, processing and interpreting data to answer a question. The data cycle (see Figure 6.4) is key to this and is stressed in the NNS. The important thing to remember is that you can start at any point in the cycle and go around more than once in an investigation. A common problem in data handling is that the children spend a very long time collecting the data, then another long time drawing graphs and colouring them in so that there is no time left for interpreting the data. It is in the interpretation of the data that the higher-order thinking comes so it is important that the children engage in this part of the cycle regularly.

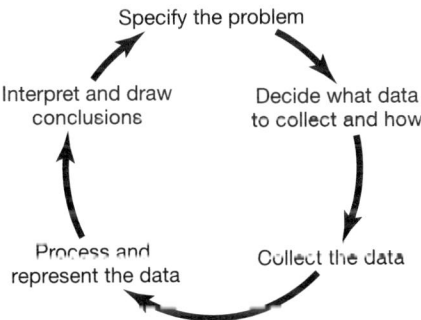

Figure 6.4 The data cycle.

Case study 6.1 Donna Young: The data cycle

I work on a daily basis in a Year 4 class supporting a small group of SEN children. The children have recently been looking at map symbols as part of their geography work and I thought that this would be a good opportunity to use data handling. I wanted the children to have input in the investigation rather than follow my suggestions. This would not only help with their decision-making skills, it would build their confidence.

It can be very easy to give SEN children too much assistance because you are eager to move their learning on, yet this could be counter-productive as they are not being given opportunities to think for themselves. Observing the children making decisions would also enable me to observe their understanding of data handling.

Our investigation included the aspects from the data cycle shown in Table 6.1.

Table 6.1

Data cycle	What I asked the children	What they said
Specify the problem	Who needs this information?	People who want to visit, so they know what's there.
Decide on what data to collect and how	What shall we choose and how shall we record it?	We can look for paths, lakes, historic buildings, golf clubs and pubs. We can do a tally chart.
Collect data	How shall we find the information?	By looking at the map.
Process and represent the data	What shall we do with our tally to show our findings?	Make a bar chart.
Interpret and draw conclusions	What can we see from our chart?	That there are lots of paths but no historic buildings. There are three pubs though! It would be a good place for people who liked walking.
Specify the problem	Might this be a problem?	You might hate walking. We would have to look at another bit of the map to see if there was more to do.

The children collaborated well during the activity, although they did need some help remembering the names for tallying and a bar chart. They called tallying, 'that thing where you make 5' and bar chart was 'those towers you make'. I was, however, satisfied from these explanations that they knew what they wanted to carry out. The group also needed help when they were completing the bar chart. They understood that you had to write numbers and the map findings somewhere, but were unsure of where and how. The activity proved to be valuable in assessing where the children's learning was at as well as giving them an opportunity, as I mentioned earlier, to participate independently in planning, collecting, representing and interpreting data as specified by the data cycle.

When children participate in data handling, they are not always given the opportunity to plan and collect. Because the children had found their own data, they appeared to be more interested in interpreting their findings than they probably would have been if they were told what to put in a chart or a graph.

TASK 6.3

HLTA 3.2.2 Monitor pupils' responses to learning tasks and modify your approach accordingly.

Think about data handling you have been involved in with children. Which parts of the data cycle were included? Which parts took up the most time? How could the higher-order thinking, the interpreting and drawing conclusions, be emphasised? See Appendix 6 for suggestions.

Discrete versus continuous data

Data handling provides excellent opportunities for cross-curricular links. The previous case study was based on geography. When choosing a free-standing data handling exercise a frequent topic is 'favourite X'. This can be favourite pet, colour, football team, food, hobby, books, etc. Related topics are 'most common X', e.g. most common shoe size, amount of pocket money, number in your family, birthday month, etc. Children enjoy collecting data about these topics but they are limiting because they always result in discrete data. Discrete data is that which can be counted rather than measured. The one axis (usually the x-axis) has labels of the categories investigated and the other axis (usually the y-axis) has numbers to indicate the frequency with which these categories occurred. With discrete data it does not matter in which order you put the items on the x-axis. You cannot use line graphs with discrete data because the points in between have no meaning.

Case study 6.2 Tamsin Nash: Constructing graphs

The children were asked to find out the favourite choice of fruit for two classes so the school would know which boxes to send to us for break (when a choice was available). This gave the children the opportunity to discuss how they were going to begin this task and after coming up with the idea of a tally chart, we started off by revision of how to go about making one.

When the information had been collected, the next question was how best to show their findings. They quickly settled on the idea of a graph but there was a disagreement on which type of graph to use. Some children wanted a line graph because it was quicker and easier but the majority wanted to present their findings in a bar chart. When asked why, the main answer was that it was a clear way of making the findings obvious. Most felt it could be made bright and colourful and thus easy to read. One child suggested that 'a line graph would give answers that were impossible as there would be a mark between fruit'. I felt this was a great explanation of the appropriate presentation of discrete versus continuous data and so the group began their charts.

When left to design their own axes, however, I was surprised at the lack of thought that some of the more able children showed. While I worked with one group discussing the best way to mark our numbers for presentation, the 'top' group got on with the task themselves. Most of the results were encouraging but it was interesting to note how one child, who usually takes great care with his work, chose an inappropriate scale, making his graph difficult to read and inaccurate. It would seem he had thought about the total number of children asked as the maximum number of fruit he may have in one column. He had not thought to use the information already collected on his tally chart to label the axis and we discussed this to bring out the learning point of planning ahead. The group I helped also thought this was the case to begin with until we discussed the issue and one of the children spotted the numbers stated in the tally chart results. They then saw how they could improve the accuracy and clarity of their graphs by utilising the space on the page. The group analysed their graph and produced some statistics for the school secretary.

The children in my group, who struggle with many aspects of numeracy, enjoyed this task and I feel there were two main reasons for this. The first is that the problems they encountered were discussed as a group beforehand, e.g. selecting the scale of the graph and designing the x-axis to show equal sized bars led to my illustrating our findings. The second was that the children recognised that the task might actually help them get a better choice of fruit in the classroom, rather than just being a series of meaningless figures.

TASK 6.4

HLTA 2.5 Know the key factors that can affect the way pupils learn.

Explore some of the difficulties children might have when drawing graphs. Make a checklist of all the things you need to think about when designing a graph, e.g. type of graph, labels, scale. How could you help children to remember these? See Appendix 6 for suggestions.

Continuous data is generally measured. The order does matter for this data and both axes generally have numbers rather than word labels. Line graphs can be used because every point on the line carries meaning even if that particular point was not measured. This data often comes from experiments in science, such as measuring length or temperature over a period of time, e.g. the height of the bean plant as it grows over several weeks or the temperature of the hot water in the insulated cup over several minutes. Although the children did not measure the temperature every minute you can use the graph to predict what the temperature would have been in the unmeasured minutes (see Figure 6.5).

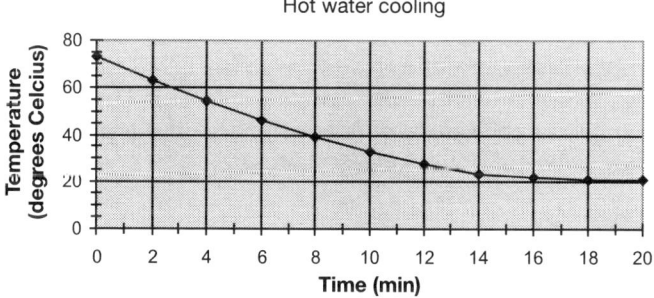

Figure 6.5 A line graph.

Continuous data can also be generated by algebraic equations, e.g. $y = 2x$. These are not often encountered in primary schools except for conversion line graphs, converting from one currency to another or from an imperial to a metric measurement.

Continuous data can result in a scattergraph with a line of best fit. Comparisons of the same two body measurements for a group of children can be used for this, such as height versus reach, to see if there is a pattern or relationship between them. From the scattergraph in Figure 6.6 you can see that a straight 'line of best fit' could be drawn that would take in most of the points while not joining them all exactly. This indicates that there is a relationship between a person's height and reach. It is important to emphasise that scattergraphs should not be treated like a dot-to-dot puzzle.

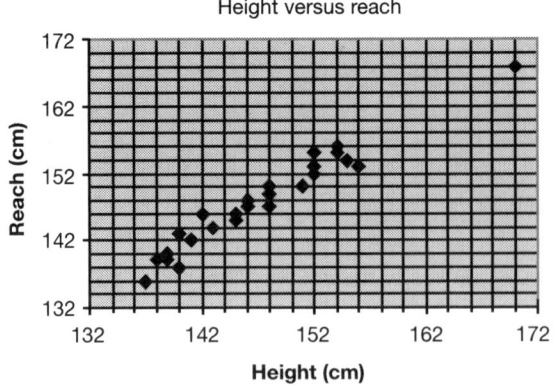

Figure 6.6 A scattergraph.

When selecting topics for discrete and continuous data you need to be careful, even with apparently easy topics such as eye colour and hair colour. It can be very difficult to determine eye colour and put it into discrete categories like blue, green, brown and hazel. Hair colour can be difficult in discrete categories also, for example deciding the dividing line between blonde and brown. However, making a continuous line of hair colour also causes problems. While you could probably organise the children from the lightest blonde to the darkest black without too much difficulty, where would you place the red heads? In addition, you need to be careful of potentially sensitive topics such as weight, pocket money, holidays, family and test scores.

> **TASK 6.5**
>
> *HLTA 3.1.1 Contribute effectively to teachers' planning and preparation of lessons.*
>
> Think of several topics for data collection. Are they discrete or continuous? Which of these would be appropriate for the children you work with?

Collecting data

Collecting data is one of children's favourite parts of data handling. Unfortunately they do not always do this efficiently; the result is data that are not very reliable and that took a very long time to collect. This can also be quite disruptive if it involves carrying out surveys in other classes. When collecting data for a 'favourite X', as discussed previously, it is important for the children to understand how many times they are allowed to vote (usually just once). Then there needs to be a system to ensure that every child votes once and only once. In Ancient Greece there were voting disks. Every eligible citizen had a voting disk and would place it in the appropriate container, which ensured that they voted only once. Today the electorate has polling cards. A similar system can be used with children, although it is simpler to use a class register or just have the children move or sit down once they have made their choice. In the following case study the children made a human graph so could only vote once.

Case study 6.3 Emma Bowden: Data handling with Foundation Stage

Within my Foundation Stage setting we have been looking at transport and roads. The children looked at the busy road outside and the cars that restrict access, especially at the beginning and end of the day. We do have a lollipop lady, but the children still thought it was busy. They were able to *specify a problem*: too many cars at the start/end.

We decided to see how the children in the class came to school. We prepared laminated pictures of cars, bikes, buses, taxis and people walking. These were laid out on the floor to represent the methods of transport and the children found a picture to represent their journey. The children were then asked to sort themselves into 'groups'.

The children moved around. Firstly two children got into a friendship group, another said they would like to come on the bus and stood with a child with that picture. It took approximately six minutes for the children to sort out the problem. A couple of children needed support to find where to go.

We then made a human pictogram, as the children stood to be counted. One child from each line was selected to count. It was important to remind the child to count themselves (quite often at this age they forget themselves). The teacher recorded the results onto the board and then suggested we print the results of our human pictogram on the computer.

I worked with small groups showing them how to make a pictogram using the 'My World' program. It is quite easy for children to click and drag the numbers and pictures. It is important to show the children that 0 is needed first. They needed support as to where the numbers and vehicles went.

An area of data handling often overlooked is 'interpret and discuss'. This is often down to the allocation of time. In the Foundation Stage we often revisit areas and look at subjects over a period of time. We produced an A3 pictogram created by a group of children on the computer. From this we were able to ask the children questions:

'How many children did we have altogether?'
'How many children walk to school?'
'How could we reduce the number of cars?'

The children were able to come up and count the pictures to answer the first two questions and came up with plausible suggestions for the third.

Using ICT

In the case study the children used a computer program to create a pictogram. There are many data handling packages available for the computer, including ones designed especially for young children to use. With these packages the children can produce a range of graphs easily which greatly reduces the amount of time spent on colouring in bar charts. They also make pie charts accessible. Pie charts are useful for demonstrating proportions or percentages rather than the actual numbers involved but are tricky to draw by hand.

Data can be entered into databases and then interrogated. Pre-existing databases can be used so that the focus is on interpreting and drawing conclusions rather than gathering data. Through the Internet many databases are readily available, such as train timetables, TV guides, supermarket prices, information about space, etc. Finding relevant data will require some research skills but is well worth it. As a millennium project a children's census was created which included information about children, compiled by children, from several countries. Since 2000 the Census at School has grown to include more countries and more topics.

> **TASK 6.6**
>
> *HLTA 2.4 Know how to use ICT to advance pupils' learning, and be able to use common ICT tools for your own and pupils' benefit.*
>
> Find out what computer programs your school has for data handling. Do an Internet search for interesting data that are relevant to your curriculum.

Probability

Probability is generally introduced in Years 5 and 6, although some 'finding all possibilities' problems, which can be used from Foundation Stage upwards, are related to it. For example, if teddy has three shirts and two pairs of trousers, how many outfits can you make for teddy? How many different meals could you choose from a three-course menu? These can be useful extension activities for able children, as is designing games or spinners to fit given probabilities.

Misconceptions abound in probability. A common misconception with children is to focus on the number rather than the proportion. For example, they believe you are more likely to pull a blue sock from a drawer of 24 socks where 12 of them are blue rather than a drawer of ten socks where six of them are blue. The opposite misconception also occurs, when children believe that you are equally likely to pull a blue sock or a white sock from the drawer containing only blue and white socks, regardless of the number of socks, because there are only two choices. Another common misconception is that a certain number or combination is less likely to occur than others. This is often believed about rolling a six when playing games with dice. The basis of this misconception is that the children remember waiting and waiting to roll a six to start a game. Many adults have strong but ill-founded beliefs about what lottery numbers to pick.

An important aspect of probability is calculating the theoretical probability of an event occurring. To do this you need to work out how many possible outcomes there are and then determine how many ways there are to achieve the desired outcome. For example, if you want to draw a heart from a pack of cards, there are 52 possible cards and 13 of them are hearts, so the probability of drawing a heart is 13/52 or 1/4 or 25 per cent. While children can understand this calculation they are then disturbed when they draw four cards and they do not get one heart. In science lessons children will often change their hypothesis to what actually happened so that they were 'right'. This predilection may affect children's understanding of probability. If the actual event is not the same as the calculated probability then they consider the calculated probability to be wrong. For example, if they roll a die six times and get 3 twos, 1 four, 1 three and 1 one, then they decide that the theoretical probability that each number is equally likely is wrong.

Some common activities for teaching about probability are experiments with coins, dice, playing cards and spinners. These are useful because it is easy to calculate theoretical probability with them and the game element is very motivating for the children. It is important to reinforce the difference between the theoretical probability and the actual results obtained.

Research summary – Teaching probability

Threlfall (2004) examined some common misconceptions in probability and then looked at whether the teaching strategies being used were helpful in combating these. He found that children use probability language in everyday contexts in a non-mathematical way. They use words like 'certain' or 'likely' to predict the outcome of events rather than to calculate the theoretical probability based on the possible outcomes.

It has been common in UK schools to ask children to order everyday statements on a probability line, whether this is divided into words such as impossible to certain or a scale from 0 to 10. However, such statements (e.g. it will rain tomorrow) are beyond the scope of children's calculations and so are responded to subjectively – what do they think is likely to happen? This tends to reinforce children's misconceptions about probability rather than focusing on the mathematics involved.

Activities that required children to calculate the probability of random events such as rolling dice, using spinners, picking cards and flipping coins demonstrated that many children could determine the appropriate fraction for a given event. However, some children would then compare two events that they had calculated as having the same theoretical probability and say that one was more likely than the other. This implies strongly that they did not have a real understanding of what the calculated probabilities meant.

Similar activities that asked children to calculate the probability and then undertake it a limited number of time, such as throwing a die ten times, were supposed to show that the theoretical probability does not necessarily happen, especially when dealing with a small sample. However, the children often believed that the calculated probability was wrong rather than draw the above conclusion about random events.

Threlfall admits that it is hard to know whether a child truly understands mathematical probability versus the subjective, everyday use of probability language. Nevertheless, he feels that reducing the amount of probability in the primary curriculum and restricting it to the older children was an appropriate decision.

> **TASK 6.7**
>
> *HLTA 2.3 Understand the aims, content, teaching strategies and intended outcomes for the lessons in which you are involved, and understand the place of these in the related teaching programme.*
>
> Preferably with a partner who works with different aged children to yourself think about your understanding of probability. Do you use probability terms with the everyday meaning or the more precise mathematical meaning? Do you understand the difference between a calculated theoretical probability and an intuitive response? How does your understanding impact on planning and teaching? Compare your experiences.

The various aspects of data handling fit well into problem-solving and the objectives related to using and applying mathematics. This will be explored further in the following chapter, not only for data handling but for all aspects of mathematics.

> **Key Points**
>
> - Sorting is the basis of data handling.
> - Children learn best when they have opportunities to use data that are meaningful to them.
> - Children need to experience the complete data cycle, especially interpreting the data and drawing conclusions.

> **Reflections**
>
> Can you think of opportunities for the children to be involved in real data handling, where the conclusions will have some impact on their lives?
>
> Why is data handling an important skill?
>
> What sort of data do you have to interpret as an adult? How is it presented?

7

Problem-solving

This chapter will help you to:

- identify different types of question
- support children during problem-solving
- find opportunities for children to solve realistic problems

Problem-solving has been saved for the final chapter because it provides the context for the issues discussed in all of the previous chapters. Teaching mathematics *through* problem-solving and realistic contexts is vitally important in developing understanding of all aspects of mathematics and a problem-solving approach should be embedded in all lessons. Problem-solving comes under the heading of Using and Applying Mathematics in the National Curriculum. Although this had been a separate section in earlier versions, the National Curriculum (1999) integrated the programme of study for Using and Applying Mathematics into Number; Shape, Space and Measures; and Data Handling to emphasise its centrality to all aspects of mathematics.

Types of problems

Problem-solving in mathematics can mean many different things. Askew and Wiliam (1995) identified four types of mathematical problems:

- *standard problems* – a word or story problem where a calculation is put into a context;
- *non-standard problems* – more complex problems where the child has to work out how to solve it;
- *'real-world' problems* – a context is presented and the child has to decide on the relevant information and then devise a mathematical model for the solution;
- *puzzles* – often more abstract and reliant on insight and unusual strategies.

In the *Problem Solving* training materials, the National Numeracy Strategy has described five types of problems (DfES, 2004b):

- *Finding all possibilities* – these have a collection of possible answers, e.g. if I have 52 pence in my pocket, what coins could I have?
- *Logic problems* – these usually consist of a series of statements with partial information from which conclusions must be drawn, e.g. Sunita is five years older than Dev, who has not started school yet. In two years she will be twice as old as him. How old are they?
- *Finding rules and describing patterns* – these are related to algebra and involve making generalisations to find a rule and describing patterns in number or shape, e.g. What is the rule for the following number pattern? 0, 1, 1, 2, 3, 5, 8, 13, 21…
- *Diagram problems and visual puzzles* – these can relate to the other categories but are presented in a visual form, e.g. in Figure 7.1 which of the nets would fold to make a cube? How many others can you design?
- *Word problems* – these are calculations set into a story context, e.g. Judith has £1.50. She would like to buy some sweets for herself and her three friends. If she buys chocolate bars at 27 pence each, how much change will she get?

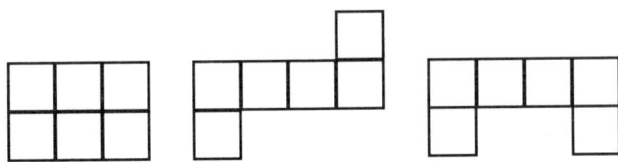

Figure 7.1 Visual puzzle.

There is some overlap with the Askew and Wiliam categories. The *Problem Solving* training materials also contain suggestions of how to support children with the different kinds of problem. With all of the problems it is important that children start by thinking about and discussing the problem to determine what it means, which information is relevant, what must be done and the most efficient way of doing it. Being systematic and organised in recording are also beneficial with most of these problems; they help to check that all possibilities have been found and make it easier to identify patterns and rules.

Research summary – Helping pupils solve problems

Fuchs et al. (2004) worked with 8- and 9-year-old children in the United States to study whether developing schemas would enhance problem-solving ability. This is based on Piaget's ideas of schemas, assimilation and accommodation. Schemas are ways that our brain organises experience in order to help us understand it. New situations are then compared to our existing schemas to see if they fit in (assimilation) or if a new schema is needed (accommodation). They taught all of the children that problem-solving involved applying their mathematical knowledge to a new situation. The children were encouraged to discuss the problems and draw diagrams to help them understand what the problem meant. They also taught them to check that their answer made sense. They would teach the children using an example problem and then provide similar problems for them to work on in pairs, followed by individual work.

Some of the classes also received teaching to create problem-solving schemas. The schemas involved classifying the problems presented into four categories. This helped the children to make connections between the new problems and ones they had already solved. One class spent ten minutes in each lesson simply sorting problems into categories. This seemed to be beneficial to the children with SEN. The results of the study showed that those children who had been taught to identify patterns and look for connections between new problems and previously solved problems with the schema training were two to three times more successful than those children who had just had the basic problem-solving instruction.

It should be noted that all four categories of problem that Fuchs et al. used would fit under the standard problem or word problem categories described above. Nevertheless, whatever categories are used to sort types of problem, the above research implies that discussing the problems, identifying their key features and connecting them to previously solved problems will be beneficial. This relates to Askew et al.'s research (1997), referred to in Chapter 2, which showed that making connections was the most effective teaching approach.

Setting mathematics into a relevant context

The Brazilian street maths study (Carraher et al., 1993) discussed in Chapter 1 showed that having a real context enabled the children to solve problems successfully. There are numerous activities in school life which can be used for problem-solving in mathematics. The following case study shows how a common school activity can be used to develop problem-solving with different age groups.

Case study 7.1 Lorna Garfoot: Pancake problem-solving

Working in a Year 2 class recently, I was able to observe the children trying to solve a problem. If there are 23 children in the class who would all like half a pancake each, and three adults who would like a whole pancake, how many pancakes do we need to make?

Although the children were working individually, conversation was encouraged, giving the less able children opportunity to be scaffolded by the more able children. The children articulated with each other, and myself, and established a variety of ways to solve the problem. Some children draw 23 half pancakes, joined them up in twos to make whole ones, then added on the three whole pancakes needed. Others drew 23 children, sharing pancakes and the teachers having a whole one.

A few children were able to use the operation of division to reach the answer:

23 children, half a pancake each, $23 \div 2 = 11\frac{1}{2}$, $11\frac{1}{2} + 3 = 14\frac{1}{2}$

Having reached the conclusion that we would need $14\frac{1}{2}$ pancakes, the more able children were able to explain that, in fact, we would have to make 15, as it was not possible to make half a pancake. The children were initially worried by the fact that a piece of pancake would remain, but had courage and the risk was diminished by like-minded peers.

A group of Year 4 children, also making pancakes, were set the problem of finding out who got the largest pancake. Much discussion took place as to whether the fairest way to judge the size of the pancakes was to weigh them, measure the diameter or work out what area they covered. It was decided that weighing them would risk them breaking on the scales. Measuring the diameter was ruled out because the pancakes were an irregular shape and they couldn't be sure to measure the correct diameter. The pupils decided the best way of measuring was to calculate the area. They did this by placing each pancake onto a sheet of greaseproof paper, drawing around it, and placing an acetate marked in centimetre squares over the drawing and counting how many squares the pancake covered. The children then collected the information in a table and presented it in graph form.

The amount of formal vocabulary used in the exercise was considerable as the children pondered over various methods of weighing and measuring. Characteristics of shapes were discussed, as they considered measuring the circumference or perimeter of the pancakes. Some children knew how to calculate the area of a square using multiplication and considered using this as part of their calculation, then realised the difficulties of measuring the remainder of the pancake and changed their minds. Once again, the discussion before the task proved vital to a successful outcome.

> **TASK 7.1**
>
> *HLTA 1.4 Work collaboratively with colleagues, and carry out their roles effectively, knowing when to seek help and advice.*
>
> Explore and make notes on opportunities for problem-solving in your school. These may come from other subjects but they could also be from wider aspects of school life such as organising the summer fair, erecting displays, putting on a show or preparing for a special assembly. Find a way of sharing these ideas with colleagues.

Cross-curricular opportunities abound in problem-solving. As a result you may be supporting mathematical thinking outside of specific mathematics lessons. The Primary National Strategy document *Excellence and Enjoyment* (2003b) promotes the use of cross-curricular planning so these opportunities ought to be identified and utilised.

Research summary – Purpose and utility

Ainley et al. (2006) suggest that mathematical activities should have both *purpose* and *utility*. The purpose is a meaningful outcome, as perceived by the pupils, while the utility is an understanding of how to apply the concept. Activities which have both purpose and utility allow children to learn through the activity, rather than merely applying knowledge after learning.

Ainley et al. suggest that role-play situations, such as shops, provide some purpose and utility but they are often simplified so that they are not realistic and the child does not have the same level of commitment to accuracy as in the real situation. A person in a real shop cannot buy things without sufficient money and cares that the amount of change received is correct! Instead, they recommend technology projects, since they have a clear end product (purpose) and the mathematics involved needs to be accurate for the project to succeed (utility). Although the purpose for the child is the end product, the teacher's purpose may have been a mathematical objective.

'Real-life problems' that are not real

As Ainley et al. (2006) noted it is difficult to find real-life contexts that are both meaningful to the child and realistic in the mathematics. Often the prices in role-play shops or post offices are set at unrealistically low levels so that they are within the mathematical scope of the children. Although the children are learning about the processes of transaction in a shop, they may also be learning that a chocolate bar costs two pence. It is possible to establish role play areas which involve small numbers in a realistic context: the old-fashioned sweet shop, the jumble sale, cake sale, second-hand toys or books. Although this could be role play, it could also involve real transactions.

> **TASK 7.2**
>
> *HLTA 3.1.3 Contribute effectively to the selection and preparation of teaching resources that meet the diversity of pupils' needs and interests.*
>
> Consider the issue of role-play situations using realistic numbers versus numbers within the children's mathematical scope. What are the advantages and disadvantages of each? Which do you think is more important? What role-play situations can you think of for older children?

'Real-life' problems may be encountered in the form of word problems as well as in role play, but we need to think about the reality of these 'real' problems. Some children in Year 3 were given the task of creating word problems for each other to solve. The example that was shared with the class was: *There are 213 pieces of rubbish on the field. The caretaker picks up 174 pieces. How many pieces of rubbish are left?*

This clearly indicates subtraction, although counting up could be used instead. However, if you think about the question more deeply there are some issues about the reality of the problem. How did anyone know there were 213 pieces of rubbish on the field? If someone had counted them why didn't they pick them up at the same time? Why did the caretaker only pick up 174 pieces? Why is there so much rubbish on the field anyway and what can be done to prevent it in the future?

Cooper and Harries (2002) studied children's responses to the reality within mathematics questions. They found that most children will merely accept the question and focus on the hidden mathematics but can be encouraged to consider the reality of the situation depending on how it is presented. They found that asking them to justify whether another child's answer could be correct or not helped the children to think more realistically about the problem. In their study they used questions similar to the following.

A Year 4 class were told that two CD towers held 30 CDs each and another two CD towers held 45 CDs each and then asked how many CDs there were altogether. Most of the children dutifully added to find the total but a high-attaining boy said that you could not know how many CDs there were. This answer confused the teacher but the teaching assistant who had been sitting near the boy and had heard him talking through his thinking with the other children on the table was able to explain what he meant. Although it is possible to calculate how many CDs *could* be held on the towers, this does not guarantee that the towers are full, so the answer could be anything from 0 to 150.

Although this child considered the reality of the situation, the following research study shows that the opposite can be true as well, that children apparently ignore the sense of the question and just focus on the calculation.

Research summary – How old is the captain?

There have been several studies, in various countries, which have asked children questions that could not be answered from the information; for example, 'A shepherd owns 19 sheep and 13 goats. How old is the shepherd?' (Selter, 1994: 34). The strange result in each of these studies was that the children used the information they had with a variety of operations in order to 'solve' the problem. Selter (1994) and a group of trainee teachers thought that these results were bizarre and would not be replicated by their children.

They designed a series of questions, some of which could be answered and some of which could not. Selter and the trainee teachers were startled to find that their children had answered all of the questions, apparently ignoring the sense involved. They decided to try again a few months later but this time they told the children that some of the questions could not be answered. In the second attempt far fewer of the children tried to answer the insolvable problems.

When they examined video tapes of the children working out the insolvable problems they found that the children were not ignoring the sense of the question. The children expressed doubts about the question and then struggled to find an approach that would give them an answer. The children would invent stories to explain their approach to answering, e.g. the shepherd had been given a sheep or a goat every year for his birthday so the total matches his age; the bee keeper could be 400 years old because he came from a different planet where they counted differently.

As well as considering the mathematics involved it is important to think about the social context. The children are used to mathematics questions in school having correct answers. Therefore, in their willingness to please the teacher, they endeavour to find an answer, whether it seems sensible to them or not.

TASK 7.3

HLTA 3.2.1 Be able to support teachers in evaluating pupils' progress through a range of assessment activities.

Observe and listen to some children solving problems. How do they approach the problem? Do they think about the sense of the question or do they just look for a calculation to undertake?

Questioning

One of the key strategies to support children's problem-solving is questioning. How children approach a problem can be influenced by the questions they are asked. In the following case study the teaching assistant asked a range of open questions to encourage the children to think and make decisions but also asked directed questions which encouraged the children to try out different ideas.

> **Case study 7.2 Katy Green: Questioning**
>
> In the nursery class in my setting the children have recently undertaken work using the nursery rhyme Humpty Dumpty. Two children of varying abilities took part in an investigation to build a wall for Humpty. The children were given a variety of resources, including spheres, prisms and cubes. The children were very enthusiastic, especially with a soft Humpty to sit on the finished wall.
>
> **Q**: Here's Humpty and he hasn't got a wall to fall off. Shall we build him a wall? Look at all these materials here; which do you think is going to make the best wall?
> **Q**: What about these? (*I showed the children the small balls/spheres.*)
> **A**: They're all balls.
> **Q**: Would that work for Humpty's wall?
> **A**: No, Humpty would roll off.
> **Q**: What would be best to make a wall?
> **A**: (*The little boy then picked up the cubes.*)
> **Q**: Do you think those bricks would make a good wall?
> **A**: (*He started to put the bricks in a row.*)
> **Q**: How could we use the cubes to make a wall for Humpty?
> **A**: I know, let's put one on top of the other. (*He then built a tower of six cubes.*)
> **Q**: Shall we try and see if Humpty fits?
> **A**: (*The tower fell down.*)
> **Q**: What could we do to make the wall stronger for Humpty?
> **A**: (*The little girl built another tower; the little boy told her that it needed to be stronger.*)
> **Q**: How can we make it stronger?
> **A**: (*The little boy then built a tower with three rows of bricks.*)
> **Q**: Shall we try Humpty on the wall?
> **A**: (*Humpty stayed on the wall. The little boy was very pleased with himself.*)
> **Q**: Is there anything we can do to make Humpty's wall better?
> **A**: We can put more bricks so that it doesn't fall down.
> **Q**: What, in a tower?
> **A**: No all around, so it doesn't fall down.

> I didn't have any firm questions prepared as working with young children can take you down many different avenues; I had a few notes for questions that I could use if we digressed. The questions helped the children to understand and develop their ideas of what would balance to make a wall.

In English closed questions are ones which can be answered with one word while open questions require longer answers. In mathematics closed questions have a single correct answer while open questions have a range of possible answers. For example, 'What do you need to add to 37 to get 100?' is closed but 'Find two numbers that add together to make 100' is open. Open questions can be less threatening to children because there are more chances of getting a correct answer. When used in problem-solving open questions can require greater analysis and understanding from the children rather than just recall of a procedure. For example, 'calculate the area of this rectangle' can be transformed into 'draw several different shapes that have an area of 12 cm^2'. The open problem allows the child to demonstrate a much higher level of attainment and requires more thought about the properties of shape rather than just remembering a formula. The terms 'problem-solving' and 'investigations' are often used interchangeably but sometimes a distinction is made between them, with problem-solving being used for closed problems and investigations used for open ended problems. Investigations can be developed further so that the children examine why the solution works rather than just stopping once a solution is found.

As well as discussing open and closed questions, the *Mathematical Vocabulary* booklet (DfEE, 2000: 4) lists a hierarchy of questions:

- *Recall of facts* – What is 3 + 7?
- *Applying facts* – If you know the 5× table, what is 50 × 6?
- *Hypothesising and predicting* – How many children do you think will fit on this bench?
- *Designing and comparing procedures* – How would you solve 19 × 99? Can you think of any other ways? Which do you find the best and why?
- *Interpreting results* – What does that tell us about adding even and odd numbers?
- *Applying reasoning* – What is the largest angle possible inside a triangle?

This hierarchy represents an increasing level of cognitive challenge. Recall of facts is the lowest level because it relies on memory rather than higher-level thinking skills.

However, the full hierarchy applies to all age groups. Recall of facts can be appropriate for nursery children (*what comes after three?*) or for A-level students (*what is the cosine of 1?*). By the same token, applying reasoning is appropriate for young children (*which of these shapes could be used to make a rocket?*). It is the level of the mathematical content within the question that makes it suitable for a particular age group.

> **TASK 7.4**
>
> *HLTA 3.2.3 Monitor pupils' participation and progress, providing feedback to teachers, and giving constructive support to pupils as they learn.*
>
> Observe a mathematics lesson and analyse the types of questions used. Are there more open or closed questions? Which part of the hierarchy of questions dominates? How do the pupils respond to the different types of question?

The following case study demonstrates how the hierarchy of questions can be planned for and how this can contribute to the problem-solving process. It also shows the benefits of collaboration.

> **Case study 7.3 Anne Marie Goode: Hierarchy of questions**
>
> *Year 3 is going on a trip. There are 11 boys, 13 girls, 1 teacher, 1 teaching assistant and 4 parent helpers. What size of bus would they need to seat everyone: a 24, 32 or 42 seater?*
>
> The aim of the task was to develop the children's problem-solving skills. Throughout the task the children were encouraged to discuss how to tackle each of the problems with each other. They were also asked a range of questions which were intended to encourage enquiry, thus contributing to the learning outcome. Upon successful completion of the activity, a number of extension questions were asked to reinforce the strategies used.
>
> - *Hypothesising and predicting* – What size of bus do you think they will need? Will the bus be full?
> - *Designing and comparing* – How many ways can we work this problem out to get the answer? How can we make the numbers easier to count? Are there other ways of doing it?
> - *Interpreting results* – So now that we know the size of the bus, are there any empty seats?
> - *Applying reasoning* – If the seats on the bus are in twos, can all the girls have a girl partner? What about the boys?
> - *Extension questions* – How many children are going? How many adults are going? How many altogether? If each child paid £1.50 for the trip, how much was collected altogether?

> It was found that the children responded well to the different types of questions and that the questions did encourage the children to discuss, or 'think aloud', the strategies they thought they should use in order to answer each question. The children worked well together, and there was a genuine sense of collaborative learning taking place throughout the task. This activity was definitely more rewarding than a worksheet activity would have been; the children appeared to enjoy the discussion aspect of the task and were more than willing to help each other out. The activity made it clear to the children that problem-solving tasks do require a number of steps to be taken before the answer can be reached. I came to the conclusion that some of these children would not have been able to solve the problems without being asked crucial questions or discussing the options with their peers.

TASK 7.5

HLTA 3.1.3 Contribute effectively to the selection and preparation of teaching resources that meet the diversity of pupils' needs and interests.

Plan some questions from the higher level of the hierarchy for your next mathematics lesson. Some examples are provided in Appendix 7.

Gifted children

Although all children can benefit from a problem-solving approach to mathematics, it is particularly useful for gifted and able children, as open-ended questions allow them to challenge themselves. The higher-order thinking skills encourage them to think deeply and apply reasoning. They require the children to search for patterns and connections and can lead to developing algebra, proof and making general statements. As well as developing thinking skills, problem-solving requires certain attitudes towards work: perseverance and adaptability. A creative approach is often needed, especially with non-standard problems. These are attitudes that are beneficial to all children, not just the gifted. Problem-solving opportunities, supported by an encouraging teaching assistant, can develop these. Mixed ability groupings can be quite effective in problem-solving, with children having to explain their thinking to each other. This can help clarify the thinking of the more able and develop the problem-solving approaches of the less able.

Magic squares are an example of a mathematical puzzle that can be used with a range of ages depending on the size, numbers involved and the extent to which it is developed. The first magic square appears to have been constructed in China, around 2800 BC. In a magic square all of the rows, columns and diagonals add up to the same total. The simplest squares are three rows by three columns, with nine spaces in all. Usually you are given a set of numbers and each number may only be used once within the square. However, magic squares for young children can involve repeated numbers. For example, put the numbers 1, 2 and 3 in the square so that all of the rows, columns and diagonals have the same total. Using the numbers 1 to 9, once each, is more challenging and is suitable for junior children. The process of finding where to place the numbers should involve hypothesising and looking for patterns. A computer can be used to make a model of a magic square that will allow the children to try out solutions without having to do the adding up. This allows the children to focus on the higher-order problem-solving skills rather than the number skills and can be a great support for children who struggle with arithmetic. Older and more able children should be encouraged to make generalised statements about the square and its solution, possibly in the form of algebra. Once the statements are made they can be tested by using a different set of numbers. Then you can explore whether the same patterns are true for 5 × 5 squares and 7 × 7 squares. What about 4 × 4 squares? It is even possible to construct a three-dimensional magic cube.

TASK 7.6

HLTA 3.1.3 Contribute effectively to the selection and preparation of teaching resources that meet the diversity of pupils' needs and interests.

Try to complete the magic square (Figure 7.2) using the numbers 1 to 9. If you find this too easy try some of the extensions suggested above. Once you have found the solution, think about how you solved it. What questions could you ask the children to help them with the problem-solving process? What resources or models could you use to help them? What would be appropriate questions or clues for children who are getting frustrated? See Appendix 7 for the solution and some suggestions.

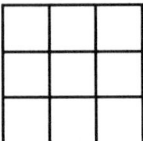

Figure 7.2 Magic square.

Problem-solving is a key component of mathematics and a key skill in life. It demonstrates the relevance of mathematics to everyday life and encourages higher-order thinking. It should not be seen as an occasional extra but as an integral part of all mathematics teaching. Supporting problem-solving involves helping children to make sense of the problem and encouraging them to be systematic in their approach. Both of these can be achieved through careful questioning.

Key Points

- Problem-solving is the application of mathematics.
- Realistic problems help children understand mathematics.
- Posing questions that challenge children can support them in problem-solving.

Reflections

How do you approach mathematical problems?

Do you find opportunities for introducing problem-solving in a variety of curriculum and wider school contexts?

Are you planning your questions to encourage higher-order thinking?

Do high-attaining children need a different kind of support to children with SEN?

How are you developing the children's understanding of how mathematics relates to the world outside school?

Appendices

The appendices are listed by chapter and contain additional information, tables and exercises to supplement the text.

Appendix 1

Task 1.1

Take a few moments to note down where you have used or encountered mathematics over the last 24 hours. This could involve calculations, making estimations, using measurements including time, handling data or working with shapes. Discuss how you have used maths knowledge most with a colleague.

Some possible areas might include the following:

- *Going to work* – reading exact times; estimating time for activities and journey; sorting and matching clothing; packing various shapes into a lunch box or bag; reading scales in the car such as speedometer and fuel gauge.
- *Cooking* – measuring capacity, mass and time; diameter; area and volume; estimating; ratio.
- *Shopping* – estimating running total; selecting appropriate money; checking change.
- *DIY/sewing* – exact measuring of lengths and angles.
- *Decorating* – exact measuring; estimating measures; multiplying.
- *Television* – extracting data from a table (TV guide).
- *Banking* – calculating to check statement.

Task 1.4

Reflect on the strategies employed in this activity (see Case study 1.1). Identify those which helped to make this a positive and accessible experience for the children.

The following are some of the strategies used:

- Using the skittles put the mathematics into the context of a game. It also made it a kinaesthetic activity which would have been more accessible to some learners.
- The children were working in small groups so each got to have a turn rolling the ball. The group was small enough to ensure everybody participated in the discussion. The small groups also allowed shyer children to contribute who would not normally speak in a whole-class situation.
- The TA asked for explanations as well as answers. This told her more about the children's thinking processes but also provided models for the other children.
- She used open-ended questions to probe the children's thinking and encourage reasoning skills.
- Allowing the children to teach her their methods raised their self-esteem and confidence.

Appendix 2

Task 2.2

Keep taking turns drawing and describing different arrangements until they are reasonably accurate.

Most students find they begin quite generally but they –

- get more and more precise about orientation of paper/base/surface and shapes;
- begin to use language of measurement;
- begin to use language of movement and direction.

Task 2.3

Make a list of all the mathematical words you can think of that could be confused with everyday words.

Some potentially confusing mathematical words:

take away	difference	product
times	prime	volume
face	property	plane

kite	net	base
regular	degree	odd
even	units	proper (fraction)
formula	constant	match
die (singular of dice)	sign	operation
change	relationship	plan
round (to the nearest …)	table	row
column	axes	origin
mean	range	mode
pair/pear	sum/some	whole/hole

Appendix 3

Task 3.3

Try these calculations mentally:

$66 - 29, 66 + 8, 309 - 77, 309 + 95, 4.08 - 1.3, 4.08 + 3.1$

$180 \div 12, 25 \times 7, 9.6 \div 0.4, 20 \times 19$

Analyse your own methods. What known facts did you use and what ideas did you apply? Would the children you work with do things the same way?

The answers to the questions are given below with some of the ways you might have solved them but many other methods are possible.

- $66 - 29 = 37$
  A common way to think about this is *compensating* so you subtract $66 - 30$ and then add 1. You might also use *near doubles* since 66 is double 33, so the answer is $33 + 4$ (the difference between 33 and 29)
- $66 + 8 = 74$
  You might use the *known fact* that $6 + 8 = 14$ and then added this to 60. Alternatively, you could partition the 8 into $4 + 4$ to *bridge through the nearest 10*, so $66 + 4 = 70; 70 + 4 = 74$.
- $309 - 77 = 232$
  You might count up using a number line image, *bridging through 10s and 100s*. $77 + 3 = 80; 80 + 20 = 100; 100 + 200 = 300; 300 + 9 = 309$; so the answer is $3 + 20 + 200 + 9 = 232$. You might *compensate* with $307 - 77$ and then add 2 or just *partition* into $300 - 70 + 9 - 7$.
- $309 + 95 = 404$
  You might *partition and recombine* to make $304 + 100 = 404$. You could also *compensate* with $309 - 100 + 5$.
- $4.08 - 1.3 = 2.78$
  It is often easier to think of decimals as money: £4.08 − £1.30. You can then count up.
- $4.08 + 3.1 = 7.18$
  Again, try changing this to money: £4.08 + £3.10. This can be *partitioned* easily into units, tenths and hundredths.

- $180 \div 12 = 15$
  If you think of this as a fraction you can remove common factors gradually. It is probably a *known fact* that 18 and 12 are both in the 6× table, so 180 and 12 both have 6 as a factor. Dividing numerator and denominator by 6 gives $180/12 = 30/2$. This leaves another *known fact*: $30 \div 2 = 15$. You might also use *known facts* such as $(12 \times 10) + (12 \times 5)$.
- $25 \times 7 = 175$
  Known facts are useful: $25 \times 4 = 100$. You could double this and *compensate*: $25 \times 8 - 25 = 200 - 25 = 175$.
- $9.6 \div 0.4 = 24$
  Changing the question by multiplying both numbers by 10 gives $96 \div 4$ which most people find easier. You could think about halving 96 and then halving that answer. You might also recognise that $80 \div 4 = 20$ and $16 \div 4 = 4$.
- $20 \times 19 = 380$
  You could *compensate* the *near double* to $20 \times 20 - 20 = 400 - 20 = 380$.

It is likely that children would not do things in the same way as you because you will be bringing past teaching and experience to bear on solving these problems. However, if you have supported maths lessons, especially at Key Stage 2, you are likely to have developed and changed your approach to include some of the taught strategies.

Task 3.4

Solve this calculation in your head: $(19 + 18) \times (72 - 67)$. Now solve it using a calculator. Analyse the difference; what knowledge, understanding and skills did you need in each case? Which method is more appropriate for you in this particular instance?

This is a frightening calculation at first sight. Solve the brackets first.

$$(19 + 18) \times (72 - 67) = 37 \times 5$$

An easy way to think about this is $37 \times 10 \div 2 = 370 \div 2 = 185$. You could also partition the 37 to get $(30 \times 5) + (7 \times 5) = 150 + 35 = 185$.

The way you solve this using a calculator will depend on whether your calculator has brackets or not. If it does then you can just key in the calculation as shown. Otherwise, you need to know that the calculations in the brackets must be done first and either recorded, put into the calculator's memory or put into your own memory before trying the final multiplication.

Task 3.5

Ask some Key Stage 2 children to choose whether to do the following questions mentally or with a calculator:

$350 + 150$; £12.95 + £17.95; $100 - 36$; £5.00 - 95p; £1.65 × 6; 50p × 3; £4.25 ÷ 8; £5.00 ÷ 25p

Look at the way the children use calculators. Do they try mental methods first? Are they always happy to accept the displayed answer? Do they estimate first to ensure the answer is sensible? Are they able to interpret the calculator display to give the answer?

Most of these questions could be done mentally with a bit of thought and possibly some jottings. Nevertheless, many people would prefer the security of using a calculator for many of them, especially since some of them look frightening initially, like the question in Task 3.4. Was there a pattern to which questions the children were willing to attempt mentally?

The children may have had some problems interpreting the calculator display with £12.95 + £17.95 and £1.65 × 6 because only one decimal place shows on the calculator. Another problem is £4.25 ÷ 8 which needs to be rounded to 53p or 54p depending on the context. For £5.00 − 95p and £5.00 ÷ 25p they needed to convert so that both were pounds or pence. With 50p × 3 they may not have recognised that 150p is £1.50.

Appendix 4

Task 4.1

Can you work out how many different multiplication facts a child will learn in their primary school career, if learning their tables up to 10 × 10, including zeros?

There are several possible answers depending on which facts you count.

- You could count all of the statements from 0 × 0 to 10 × 10 in a multiplication square or in individual multiplication tables which gives 121 facts (see Figure A4.1).

	0	1	2	3	4	5	6	7	8	9	10
0	0	0	0	0	0	0	0	0	0	0	0
1	0	1	2	3	4	5	6	7	8	9	10
2	0	2	4	6	8	10	12	14	16	18	20
3	0	3	6	9	12	15	18	21	24	27	30
4	0	4	8	12	16	20	24	28	32	36	40
5	0	5	10	15	20	25	30	35	40	45	50
6	0	6	12	18	24	30	36	42	48	54	60
7	0	7	14	21	28	35	42	49	56	63	70
8	0	8	16	24	32	40	48	56	64	72	80
9	0	9	18	27	36	45	54	63	72	81	90
10	0	10	20	30	40	50	60	70	80	90	100

Total facts: 121

Figure A4.1 Full multiplication square.

98 SUPPORTING NUMERACY

- However, because of *commutivity* 2 × 5 = 5 × 2. Instead of having to learn the whole multiplication square you only need to learn a multiplication right-angled triangle (see Figure A4.2). This reduces the number of facts by nearly half to 66.

	0	1	2	3	4	5	6	7	8	9	10
0	0	0	0	0	0	0	0	0	0	0	0
1	0	1	2	3	4	5	6	7	8	9	10
2	0	2	4	6	8	10	12	14	16	18	20
3	0	3	6	9	12	15	18	21	24	27	30
4	0	4	8	12	16	20	24	28	32	36	40
5	0	5	10	15	20	25	30	35	40	45	50
6	0	6	12	18	24	30	36	42	48	54	60
7	0	7	14	21	28	35	42	49	56	63	70
8	0	8	16	24	32	40	48	56	64	72	80
9	0	9	18	27	36	45	54	63	72	81	90
10	0	10	20	30	40	50	60	70	80	90	100

Total facts: 66

Figure A4.2 Shaded multiplication square accounting for commutative facts.

- You might reduce this even further by thinking that 0 × anything = 0 and count this as one fact (see Figure A4.3). That brings the total down to 56.

	0	1	2	3	4	5	6	7	8	9	10
0	0	0	0	0	0	0	0	0	0	0	0
1	0	1	2	3	4	5	6	7	8	9	10
2	0	2	4	6	8	10	12	14	16	18	20
3	0	3	6	9	12	15	18	21	24	27	30
4	0	4	8	12	16	20	24	28	32	36	40
5	0	5	10	15	20	25	30	35	40	45	50
6	0	6	12	18	24	30	36	42	48	54	60
7	0	7	14	21	28	35	42	49	56	63	70
8	0	8	16	24	32	40	48	56	64	72	80
9	0	9	18	27	36	45	54	63	72	81	90
10	0	10	20	30	40	50	60	70	80	90	100

Total facts: 56

Figure A4.3 Shaded multiplication square accounting for commutative facts and 0 × anything = 0 as one fact.

- You could also consider that 1 × anything = itself and count this as one fact (see Figure A4.4). That makes the total 47.

	0	1	2	3	4	5	6	7	8	9	10
0	0	0	0	0	0	0	0	0	0	0	0
1	0	1	2	3	4	5	6	7	8	9	10
2	0	2	4	6	8	10	12	14	16	18	20
3	0	3	6	9	12	15	18	21	24	27	30
4	0	4	8	12	16	20	24	28	32	36	40
5	0	5	10	15	20	25	30	35	40	45	50
6	0	6	12	18	24	30	36	42	48	54	60
7	0	7	14	21	28	35	42	49	56	63	70
8	0	8	16	24	32	40	48	56	64	72	80
9	0	9	18	27	36	45	54	63	72	81	90
10	0	10	20	30	40	50	60	70	80	90	100

Total facts: 47

Figure A4.4 Shaded multiplication square accounting for commutative facts and 0 × anything = 0 and 1 × anything = itself as single facts.

You can see that by learning a few rules about multiplication you can greatly reduce the number of facts you need to learn. This is particularly useful for children who have difficulty remembering things. Knowing the multiplication facts is important because it makes calculations much simpler. Looking for patterns in the tables (such as the 5× table always ends in 5 or 0) is another way of helping children learn them.

Appendix 5

Task 5.2

Think about how you show shapes to children. Do you always show them in the same orientation? Do you always show the same kind? Are your triangles always equilateral? Do you ever show very long, thin oblongs? Think of ways in which you can enrich children's experience of shape.

Ways in which you can enrich children's experience of shape might include:

- going for a 'shape walk' around the school or outside;
- devising a maths trail;
- initiating cross-curricular activities such as origami in art, Rangoli patterns in RE, constructing with shapes in design & technology;
- playing games such as 'guess the shape' by giving properties one by one.

Task 5.4

Try this activity with a colleague. Imagine a square (all four sides the same length, all angles 90°). Now imagine a second square, the same size as the first, next to the first so that they share a side (no overlap). What shape do you have now? Does it matter where you put the second square? Bring on a third square the same size so that it shares a common side with one of the others. What shape do you have now? Does it matter where you put it? Now imagine a fourth square the same size as the others and join it to one of the sides of your shape. What shape do you have now?

See Figure A5.1 for possible arrangements at each stage.

Figure A5.1 Visualisation of squares.

Task 5.5

How would you describe your location at this moment? How many different ways can you find to describe it? Ask some children in the classroom to describe their position. Can you encourage them to think of different ways?

You might describe your location geographically (at a specific address, in a city, in a country); using prepositions (beside, next to, in front of, behind); using latitude and longitude; using compass points; using measurements.

Children's understanding of location and position is affected by:

- not understanding that to describe position you must have a reference point to start with;
- not having developed an understanding of how to represent 3D in a 2D perspective;
- representing things as they recognise them rather than as they are actually seeing them, making maps and plans difficult to appreciate.

Task 5.7

What are the standard units for these aspects of measures: length, capacity, weight, time, temperature? Find items which can serve as benchmarks for each of these units. What sort of clothes would you wear for 0°C, 10°C, 20°C and 30°C?

The main metric measures are:

- *Length*: millimetres (mm); centimetres (cm); metres (m); kilometres (km)
  Benchmark: doorhandles are about 1 m above the ground
- *Capacity*: millilitres (ml); centilitres (cl); litres (l)
  Benchmark: a bottle of wine is usually 75 cl or 750 ml
- *Weight*: milligrams (mg); grams (g); kilograms (kg); tonnes (t)
  Benchmark: a bag of sugar is 1 kg
- *Temperature*: degrees Celsius; 0°C – freezing point of water; 100°C – boiling point of water
  Clothing for 0°C: winter coat, scarf, gloves, jumper, hat
  Clothing for 10°C: jacket, long sleeves or sweatshirt
  Clothing for 20°C: shirtsleeves
  Clothing for 30°C: shorts and t-shirt
- *Time*: seconds (s); minutes (min); hours (hr); days; decades; years; centuries
  Time is not metric (which is base 10) but is partially base 60.

Appendix 6

Task 6.3

Think about data handling you have been involved in with children. Which parts of the data cycle were included? Which parts took up the most time? How could the higher-order thinking, the interpreting and drawing conclusions, be emphasised?

Collecting the data and drawing the graphs take up the most time. Using ICT to present the data can speed things up if the children are familiar with the technology. To ensure time for higher-order thinking you can start the data cycle at the interpreting stage by providing data such as Children's Census information, television guides, train timetables, results from science experiments. The children can then draw conclusions which may lead to new data collection.

Task 6.4

Explore some of the difficulties children might have when drawing graphs. Make a checklist of all the things you need to think about when designing a graph, e.g. type of graph, labels, scale. How could you help children to remember these?

Graph questions:

- Is the data continuous or discrete?
- What is the most appropriate type of graph (pictogram, block graph, bar chart, line graph, scattergraph or pie chart)? Why?
- What are the biggest and smallest numbers? Should you start from 0? What would be an appropriate scale?
- What is the data about? What should the label on the x-axis/bottom be?
- What units of measurement are you using? Have you marked this on the y-axis?
- Does the order of the data matter?
- What title should your graph have?
- Would someone understand what this is about if they couldn't talk to you about it?

Asking these questions of the children as they are working should help them remember all of the steps. You might be able to create a mnemonic with the children for the steps they tend to forget. Notating a completed graph with the important features can also help.

Appendix 7

Task 7.5

Plan some questions from the higher level of the hierarchy for your next mathematics lesson.

Here are some questions based on the magic square activity in Task 7.6.

- Hypothesising and predicting:
  - What do you think the total will be?
  - What number do you think should go in the middle? Why?
  - Do you think there will be any patterns?
  - Do you think this will be easy or hard? Why?
- Designing and comparing procedures:
  - What should we do first?
  - Will any resources help us?
  - How will you keep track of the solutions you've tried already?
- Interpreting results:
  - What patterns have you found?
  - What does that tell us about adding even and odd numbers?
  - Why is 5 in the middle?
    How is the total related to the middle number? Why?
- Applying reasoning:
  - Is it possible to have a different arrangement for a 3 × 3 square?
  - Could you use a different set of numbers in a 3 × 3 square?
  - How can the patterns from the 3 × 3 square help us solve a 5 × 5 square?
  - Will a 4 × 4 square have the same patterns?

Task 7.6

Try to complete the magic square (Figure 7.2) using the numbers 1 to 9. If you find this too easy, try some of the extensions suggested [in the text]. Once you have found the solution, think about how you solved it. What questions could you ask the children to help them with the problem-solving process? What resources or models could you use to help them? What would be appropriate questions or clues for children who are getting frustrated?

See Figure A7.1 for a completed magic square.

Suggested resources:

104 SUPPORTING NUMERACY

8	1	6
3	5	7
4	9	2

Figure A7.1 Completed magic square.

- A spreadsheet version of the magic square (see Figure A7.2 for formulae) will allow the children to try out numbers and see immediately whether the totals are all the same. This lets the child focus on the problem-solving rather than the arithmetic.
- Number cards 1–9 will let the children try out different solutions without having to record and erase.

	A	B	C	D
1				=A4+B3+C2
2				=A2+B2+C2
3				=A3+B3+C3
4				=A4+B4+C4
5	=A2+A3+A4	=B2+B3+B4	=C2+C3+C4	=A2+B3+C4

Figure A7.2 Formulae for a spreadsheet magic square.

- Cuisenaire rods for 1 to 9, several of each, will help the children see which totals you can make with three different rods.
- Provide a partially completed square.
- Give the children a completed 3 × 3 square and ask them to analyse the patterns, then try to make a new arrangement for 3 × 3 or try a 5 × 5 square.

Suggested questions and clues:

- Which position in the square is in the most sums?
- Which positions are in the fewest sums?
- What should the biggest number be paired with?

- What do you think the total might be?
- Why couldn't the total be 6? Or 24?
- Do you notice anything about the odd and even numbers?
- 5 goes in the middle.
- The total is 15.
- What ways do you know to make 10 with two numbers?

References

Ainley, J., Pratt, D. and Hansen, A. (2006) 'Connecting engagement and focus in pedagogic task design', *British Educational Research Journal*, 32 (1): 23–38.

Alexander, R., Rose, J. and Woodhead, C. (1992) *Curriculum Organisation and Classroom Practice in Primary Schools*. London: DES.

Antell, S.E. and Keating, D.P. (1983) 'Perception of numerical invariance in neonates', *Child Development*, 54: 695–701.

Askew, M. and Wiliam, D. (1995) *Recent Research in Mathematics Education 5–16*. London. Office for Standards in Education.

Askew, M., Brown, M., Johnson, D., Rhodes, V. and Wiliam, D. (1997) *Effective Teachers of Numeracy*. London: TTA.

Berry, J. and Picker, S. (2000) 'Your pupil's images of mathematicians and mathematics', *Mathematics in School*, March: 24–6.

Bills, C. (1999) 'What was in your head when you were thinking that?', *Mathematics Teaching*, 168: 39–41.

Black, P. and Harrison, C. (2001) 'Feedback in questioning and marking: the science teacher's role in formative assessment', *School Science Review*, 82 (301): 55–61.

Burger, W. and Shaughnessy, J. (1986) 'Characterising the Van Hiele levels of development in geometry', *Journal for Research in Mathematics Education*, 17 (1): 31–48.

Carraher, D., Nunes, T. and Schliemann, A. (1993) *Street Mathematics and School Mathematics*. Cambridge: Cambridge University Press.

Carruthers, E. and Worthington, M. (2003) *Making Sense of Mathematical Graphics: The development of understanding abstract symbolism*. Paper presented at the European Early Childhood Education Research Association's 2003 Annual Conference University of Strathclyde, Glasgow, Scotland.

Chambers, D. (1983) 'Stereotypic images of the scientist: the Draw A Scientist Test', *Science Education*, 67 (2): 255–65.

Cockcroft, W. (1982) *Mathematics Counts: Report of the committee of inquiry into the Teaching of Mathematics in Schools under the chairmanship of Dr W. H. Cockcroft*. London: HMSO.

Cooper, B. and Harries, T. (2002) 'Children's responses to contrasting "realistic" mathematics problems', *Educational Studies in Mathematics*, 49: 1–23.

Cotton, K. (1988) *Classroom Questioning*. NW Regional Educational Laboratory. Available at: http://www.nwrel.org/scpd/sirs/3/cu5.html.

DFE (1995) *Key Stages 1 and 2 of the National Curriculum*. London: HMSO.

DfEE (1999) *The National Numeracy Strategy Framework for Teaching*. London: DfEE.

DfEE (2000) *Mathematical Vocabulary*. London: DfEE.

DfEE/QCA (1999) *The National Curriculum*. London: DfEE & QCA.

DfES (2003a) *Speaking, Listening, Learning: Working with children in KS1 and KS2*. London: DFES.

DfES (2003b) *Excellence and Enjoyment: A strategy for primary schools*. DfES: London.

DfES (2004b) *Problem Solving: A CPD pack to support the learning and teaching of mathematical problem solving*. London: DfES. (Ref: DfES 0248–2004 G).

Fuchs, L., Fuchs, D., Prentice, K., Hamlett, C., Finelli, R. and Courey, S. (2004) 'Helping pupils classify and tackle mathematics problems', *Journal of Educational Psychology*, 96 (4): 635–47.

Gelman, R. and Butterworth, B. (2005) 'Number and language: how are they related?', *Trends in Cognitive Science*, 9 (1): 6–10.

Gelman, R. and Gallistel, C. (1978) *The Child's Understanding of Number*. Cambridge, MA: Harvard University Press.

Gelman, R. and Gallistel, C. (2004) 'Language and the origin of numerical concepts', *Science*, 306: 441–3.

Goulding, M. (2000) *Learning to Teach Mathematics*. London: David Fulton.

Henderson, A., Came, F. and Brough, M. (2003) *Working with Dyscalculia*. Marlborough: Learning Works.

Kyriacou, C. (2005) 'The impact of daily mathematics lessons in England on pupil confidence and competence in early mathematics: a systematic review', *British Journal of Educational Studies*, 53 (2): 168–86.

Moseley, D., Higgins, S., Bramald, R., Hardman, F., Miller, J., Mroz, M., Tse, H., Newton, D., Thompson, I., Williamson, J., Halligan, J., Bramald, S., Newton, L., Tymms, P., Henderson, B. and Stout, J. (1999) *Ways forward with ICT effective pedagogy using information and communications technology for literacy and numeracy in primary schools*. Available at: http://www.ncl.ac.uk/ecls/research/project_ttaict/TTA_ICT.pdf.

Mullis, I., Martin, M., Gonzalez, E. and Chrostowski, S. (2004) *Trends in Mathematics and Science Study 2003*. Boston: TIMSS International Study Center.

Mullis, I., Martin, M., Beaton, A., Gonzalez, E., Kelly, D. and Smith, T. (1998) *Mathematics Achievement in the Primary School Years*. Boston: TIMSS International Study Center.

Price, R. and Raiker, A. (1999) *Teacher Confidence and Teaching and Learning in Data Handling*. London: Teacher Training Agency.

QCA (1999a) *Teaching Mental Calculation Strategies: Guidance for Teachers at Key Stage 1 and 2*. Sudbury: QCA.

QCA (1999b) *Teaching Written Calculations: Guidance for Teachers at Key Stage 1 and 2*. Sudbury: QCA. (Ref: QCA/99/486)

Raiker, A. (2002) 'Spoken language and mathematics', *Cambridge Journal of Education*, 32 (1): 45–60.

Reynolds, D. and Muijs, D. (1999) 'The effective teaching of mathematics: a review of research', *School Leadership & Management*, 19 (3): 273–88.

Ruthven, K. (1998) 'The use of mental, written and calculator strategies of numerical computation by upper primary pupils within a "calculator aware number" curriculum', *British Educational Research Journal*, 24 (1): 21–42.

SCAA (1997) *The Use of Calculators at Key Stages 1–3*. London: SCAA.

Selter, C. (1994) 'How old is the captain?', *Strategies*, 5 (1): 34–7.

Shuard, H. and Rothery, A. (1984) *Children Reading Mathematics*. London: John Murray.

Shuard, H., Walsh, A., Goodwin, J. and Worcester, V. (1991) *Calculators, Children and Mathematics*. London: Simon & Schuster.

Skemp, R. (1989) *Mathematics in the Primary School*. London: Routledge.

Tanner, H. and Jones, S. (2000) *Becoming a Successful Teacher of Mathematics*. London: Routledge.

Thompson, I. (ed.) (1999) *Issues in Teaching Numeracy in Primary Schools*. Buckingham: Open University Press.

Threlfall, J. (2004) 'Uncertainty in mathematics teaching: the National Curriculum experiment in teaching probability to primary pupils', *Cambridge Journal of Education*, 34 (3): 297–314.

Further reading

For more information about teaching mathematics and learning mathematics the following titles will be helpful.

Anghileri, J. (2001) *Principles and Practices in Arithmetic Teaching*. Buckingham: Open University Press.
Berger, A., Morris, D. and Portman, J. (2000) *Implementing the Numeracy Strategy for Pupils with Learning Difficulties*. London: David Fulton.
Cooke, H. (2001) *Passport to Professional Numeracy*. London: David Fulton.
DfES (2004a) *Mathematics Module: Induction training for teaching assistants in primary schools*. London: DfES. (Ref: DfES/0572/2004)
Frobisher, L., Monaghan, J., Orton, A., Orton, J., Roper, T. and Threlfall, J. (1999) *Learning to Teach Number*. Cheltenham: Stanley Thornes.
Gates, P. (ed.) (2001) *Issues in Mathematics Teaching*. London: Routledge/ Farmer.
Goulding, M. (2004) *Learning to Teach Mathematics in the Secondary School*. London: Fulton.
Haylock, D. (2006) *Mathematics Explained for Primary Teachers*. London: Sage.
Headington, R. (1997) *Supporting Numeracy*. London: David Fulton.
Koshy, V. (1999) *Effective Teaching of Numeracy*. London: Hodder & Stoughton.
Mooney, C., Ferrie, L., Fox, S., Hansen, A. and Wrathmell, R. (2000) *Primary Mathematics: Knowledge and understanding*. Exeter: Learning Matters.
Nunes, T. and Bryant, P. (1996) *Children Learning Mathematics*. Oxford: Blackwell.
Suggate, J., Davis, A. and Goulding, M. (2001) *Mathematical Knowledge for Primary Teachers*. London: David Fulton.
Williams, S. and Goodman, S. (2000) *Helping Young Children with Maths*. London: Hodder & Stoughton.

Index

addition, 28–9, 39, 40–2, 94–5
Askew, 23, 79–80, 81

calculators, 32–4, 95, 96
   Calculator Aware Number (CAN)
      project, 32–3
Cockcroft Report, 13, 17, 24–5
common errors, 13, 15, 16, 17, 21, 23, 37,
   38, 44, 46, 47, 60, 67, 74, 75, 76, 77,
   85, 100
counting, 13–14, 36–8, 42–3
cross-curricular links, 47, 57, 58–9, 64, 71,
   73, 83, 98

data handing,
   data cycle, 69–71, 75, 101
   graphs, 70, 72, 73, 75, 101
   probability, 76–8
   sorting, 52, 66–9
   tallying, 70
decimals, 31–2, 47
diagrams,
   branch, 69
   Carroll and Venn, 67–8
discussion/oral, 8, 12–13, 18, 19, 21, 22,
   25, 26, 27, 33, 54, 89
division, 23, 27, 31–2, 45–6

estimation, 14, 27, 34, 61

fractions, 23, 47–8, 76, 82

Gelman, 14, 37
gifted/high attaining, 16, 19, 66, 76, 89–90

ICT, 10, 58, 69, 75–6, 90, 103
   ITP, 10, 21, 30, 58, 61
   Logo, 16
   see also calculators

mathematical understanding,
   cognitive styles, 3–4
   connectionist, 4, 23, 81
   functional, 3
   instrumental, 3
   relational, 3
maths trails, 54, 98
measures, 60, 82, 92, 100
   area and perimeter, 61, 62, 82
   capacity and volume, 60, 62–3
   conservation, 60, 63
   length, 60, 61
   time, 16, 28, 63
   weight and mass, 60, 63
mental images, 20, 30, 60, 99
mental methods, 24, 26, 27, 28, 34–5, 95,
   96
   improving your own, 31, 32, 34, 94–5
multiplication, 27, 31, 40–2, 44, 46, 95,
   96–8

National Numeracy Strategy (NNS), 2,
   9–10, 12, 25, 28, 30
   Daily Mathematics Lesson (DML) / three
      part lesson, 19, 22, 25
number lines, 27, 28, 30, 39
number operation laws, 40
   associative law, 28, 41
   commutative law, 28, 40, 97–8
   distributive law, 41

numbers, types of,
  cardinal, 36
  counting, 37
  natural, 37
  nominal, 36
  ordinal, 36

place value, 17, 38
percentages, 47, 76
perceptions of maths / mathematicians, 6–7, 12, 65
problem-solving, 62, 79–81, 82, 87–9, 90, 102–4

questions / questioning, 8, 25, 29, 31–2, 66, 85, 86–9, 93, 102, 103
  ways of answering, 19, 25–6

Raiker, 18, 66
ratio and proportion, 47–9
real-life maths, 2–3, 5–6, 8, 45, 47–8, 54, 55, 57, 60, 63, 72, 74, 75, 79, 81–5, 92
recording, 21–2
  informal / jottings, 22, 24, 30, 39

shape, 98
  2D, 15–16, 50–3, 56, 99
  3D/polyhedra, 50–1, 55–6, 86
  classification, 15–16, 50–2
  Van Hiele model of geometric thought, 59
space, 100
  co-ordinates, 58
  movement, 57
  tessellation, 56
Skemp, 3
Special Educational Needs (SEN), 20, 30, 70, 81
standard algorithms, 24, 30, 40
strategies, 27, 28
  bridging, 28, 39, 94
  chunking, 45–6
  compensating, 28–9, 94–5
  counting on and back, 30, 31, 40
  doubling and halving, 28, 39, 95
  partitioning, 28, 39, 94
  using known facts, 25, 27, 28, 94–5
subtraction, 13, 43, 45, 94–5
symmetry, 57

talking partners, 19, 26

vocabulary, 13, 50–1, 56, 60, 63, 82, 93–4
  categories, 17
  planning for, 18–19
  problems 15–16, 17, 44, 77

THE LIBRARY
CITY COLLEGE PLYMOUTH